The Household Economy Approach

A guide for programme planners and policy-makers

Penny Holzmann, with Tanya Boudreau,
Julius Holt and Mark Lawrence (FEG Consulting),
and Michael O'Donnell (Save the Children)

We're the world's independent children's rights organisation. We're outraged that millions of children are still denied proper healthcare, food, education and protection and we're determined to change this.

Save the Children UK is a member of the International Save the Children Alliance, working to change children's lives in more than 100 countries.

Published by
Save the Children
1 St John's Lane
London EC1M 4AR
UK
+44 (0)20 7012 6400
savethechildren.org.uk

Registered Company No. 178159

First published 2008

© Save the Children Fund and FEG Consulting 2008

ISBN 978 1 84187 119 6

This publication is copyright, but may be reproduced by any method without fee or prior permission for teaching purposes, but not for resale. For copying in any other circumstances, prior written permission must be obtained from the publisher, and a fee may be payable.

Cover photo: Boris Heger. Girls in a field in the northern highlands of Ethiopia, where Save the Children runs cash-for-work and nutrition programmes.

Edited by Jane Carroll

Typeset by Grasshopper Design Company
Printed by Biddles Ltd

Save the Children publications are printed on paper sourced from sustainable forests.

Contents

List of figures — v
List of tables — vi
Acknowledgements — vii
Abbreviations — ix
Glossary — xi

1	**Introduction to the guide**	1
1.1	About the toolkit	1
1.2	About the guide	2

2	**What is HEA?**	3
2.1	Why did HEA come about?	3
2.2	What is HEA?	4
2.3	The steps of the HEA framework	9
2.4	The baseline: steps 1 to 3	11
2.5	Outcome analysis: steps 4 to 6	21

3	**How has HEA been used?**	29
3.1	Using HEA in the design of early warning and monitoring systems	32
3.2	Using HEA in contingency and response planning	37
3.3	Using HEA in needs assessments	41
3.4	Using HEA to inform approaches to poverty reduction	47
3.5	Using HEA in the planning of social protection programmes	53
3.6	Using HEA to help identify market support interventions	65
3.7	Using HEA in project design, monitoring and evaluation	68

4	**How is HEA done?**	**73**
4.1	How is HEA information collected?	74
4.2	Storing information: HEA spreadsheets	82
4.3	Is HEA always done in the same way?	84
4.4	What does HEA require in terms of resources?	90
5	**Is HEA reliable?**	**93**
5.1	Why is HEA information collected through rapid appraisal?	93
5.2	Representativeness: questions of sampling	95
5.3	Can key informants and focus groups provide useful quantitative data?	96
5.4	Rigour, verification and bias	97
6	**Looking forward and outward: links to other approaches and issues**	**101**
6.1	How HEA links to other approaches and systems	102
6.2	How HEA links to other areas of inquiry	107
6.3	How HEA can contribute to particular issues	114
7	**Limits and criticisms of HEA**	**123**
8	**What are the products of HEA and how can they be used?**	**134**
8.1	Products from an outcome analysis	134
8.2	Products from an HEA baseline	137

Appendix: HEA timeline	140
Endnotes	142

List of figures

Figure 1: The HEA analytical framework – a simplified illustration — 7

Figure 2: The six steps of the HEA framework — 10

Figure 3: Example of a livelihood zone map: the Limpopo Basin, Mozambique — 12

Figure 4: Example of a wealth breakdown: Chongwe-Nyimba Plateau Valley Livelihood Zone, Zambia — 14

Figure 5: Baseline data from West Zambezi Livelihood Zone, Zambia — 17

Figure 6: Seasonal calendar – West Zambezi LZ, Zambia — 19

Figure 7: Livelihoods protection and survival thresholds — 28

Figure 8: The rising costs of household expenditure baskets in Harare, September 2001 compared with May 2001 — 36

Figure 9: Scenario projections in Serbia, 2000 — 40

Figure 10: Patterns of food access for households in Mashonaland, Zimbabwe — 43

Figure 11: Income levels of four wealth groups in affected districts pre-earthquake, Pakistan — 45

Figure 12: Comparison of income and expenditure among female-headed, labour-poor households in Tigray, Ethiopia — 52

Figure 13: The food deficit arising among poor households if aid to Turkana were suspended — 55

Figure 14: Two possible safety net levels — 56

Figure 15: Possible effect of additional acre of land on income and expenditure of poor households — 60

Figure 16: Expenditure patterns (in Djibouti francs) of very poor urban households – Djibouti 2001 — 61

Figure 17: Potential impact of a marketing intervention on household food access — 62

Figure 18: Cost of secondary education for one child as a proportion of annual income in Singida — 64

Figure 19: Potential household returns on an investment in market infrastructure — 67

Figure 20: Changes in wealth breakdown in Dabano, Tigray between 1970/71 and 2000/01 — 71

Figure 21: Using HEA to help identify project thresholds — 72

Figure 22: When and why calculations are done in a baseline — 81

Figure 23: Interpolating income differences within wealth groups – Hargeisa, 2003 — 88

Figure 24: How market analysis fits into the HEA framework — 111

Figure 25: Comparing poverty using 'food income' — 117

Figure 26: Comparing poverty using 'maximum access' — 118

Figure 27: HIV and AIDS and the household economy — 120

List of tables

Table 1: Methodological requirements in relation to core questions for programme planning — 4

Table 2: Problem specification for Thyolo and Mulanje Livelihood Zone, Malawi 2004 — 23

Table 3: Translation of production and macroeconomic hazards into problem specifications — 24

Table 4: Where has HEA been used? — 30

Table 5: Uses of HEA and examples of different applications — 30

Table 6: Implications for programming arising from the HEA analysis in Pakistan — 46

Table 7: Implications for poverty reduction measures arising from HEA analysis in Pakistan — 49

Table 8: How information is gathered for each step in HEA — 75

Table 9: Advantages of the baseline storage sheet — 83

Table 10: Human resources required for livelihood zoning and baseline assessment on a regional or national level — 91

Table 11: Cross-checks carried out on HEA information to ensure quality control — 99

Table 12: What HEA does not provide — 124

Table 13: Products of HEA — 135

Table 14: Limpopo Basin, Mozambique: Targeted conclusions from thematic briefs — 136

Acknowledgements

The Toolkit on the Household Economy Approach, of which this guide is one component, was co-financed by the Regional Hunger and Vulnerability Programme (RHVP), Save the Children and FEG Consulting. Thanks are due to Gary Sawdon of RHVP for the support he has given to this initiative from the outset.

Many thanks to RHVP, Stephen Devereux, Heather Kindness, Nisar Majid, Charles Rethman, Gary Sawdon, Anna Taylor and Karen Tibbo for their valuable comments.

This guide updates and replaces Save the Children's *The Household Economy Approach: A resource manual for practitioners* (2000) by John Seaman, Paul Clarke, Tanya Boudreau and Julius Holt, and also draws on resources produced subsequently by FEG Consulting.

Finally, the unsung heroes of this guide are those international and national field workers who have spent long weeks and months in the field talking to villagers and key informants and diligently piecing together the story of poor people's lives. They have pioneered new ways of obtaining and analysing HEA data in order to find the best way of helping the people they talk to. This guide is a product of their labours.

About RHVP

RHVP is a regional programme working primarily in six southern African countries (Lesotho, Malawi, Mozambique, Swaziland, Zambia and Zimbabwe) to improve short- and longer-term responses to hunger and vulnerability. It is funded by the UK's Department for International Development (DFID) and Australian Aid (AusAid). It provides support to policy-makers and practitioners, working with international, regional and national partners to maximise impact.

About FEG Consulting

FEG has been on the leading edge of livelihoods-based food security and early warning analysis, which over time has evolved from a more narrow food-needs perspective to a broader development support vision using the Household Economy Analysis (HEA) analytical framework. FEG integrates decision-makers' specific needs through this framework to guide outputs and monitor activities at project, programme and policy levels.

Abbreviations

AAH	Action Against Hunger
CAP	Consolidated Appeals Process
CCZ	Consumer Council of Zimbabwe
CFSVA	Comprehensive Food Security and Vulnerability Assessment
DFID	Department for International Development
DRC	Democratic Republic of Congo
EPA	Extension Planning Area
FAO	Food and Agricultural Organization
FEWS NET	United States Agency for International Development (USAID) Famine Early Warning System
HEA	Household Economy Approach
IDPs	Internally displaced persons
IDS	Institute of Development Studies
IHM	Individual Household Model
IPC	Integrated Phase Classification
LZ	Livelihood Zone
MLVP	Market-led Livelihoods for Vulnerable Populations
MVAC	Malawi Vulnerability Assessment Committee
NGO	Non-governmental organisation
ODI	Overseas Development Institute
PPA	Participatory Poverty Appraisal
REST	Relief Society of Tigray

RHVP	Regional Hunger and Vulnerability Programme
SADC	Southern Africa Development Community
SENAC	Strengthening Emergency Needs Assessment Capacity
SLF	Sustainable Livelihoods Framework
VAC	Vulnerability Assessment Committee
USAID	United States Agency for International Development
WFP	World Food Programme

Glossary

Analysis spreadsheet
A spreadsheet used to carry out the **outcome analysis**. There are two types: the single zone spreadsheet, used to prepare scenarios for a single livelihood zone, and the integrated spreadsheet, used for the analysis of larger geographical areas of up to 12 livelihoods zones.

Baseline
The quantified analysis of sources of food and income and of expenditure for households in each wealth group over a defined reference period.

Baseline storage sheet
A spreadsheet that enables field teams to enter, check and analyse individual interview data in the field, and to analyse and summarise field data during the interim and final data analysis sessions.

Chronic food insecurity
A household is chronically food insecure when it consistently fails to meet its minimum energy requirements.

Coping capacity
The capacity of households to diversify and expand access to various sources of food and income, and thus to cope with a specified hazard.

Hazard
A shock such as drought, flood, conflict or market disfunction that is likely to have an impact on people's livelihoods

Household
A group of people, each with different abilities and needs, who live together most of the time and contribute to a common economy, and share the food and other income from this.

Household economy
The sum of ways in which a household acquires its income, its savings and asset holdings, and by which it meets its food and non-food needs.

● THE HOUSEHOLD ECONOMY APPROACH

Livelihood protection threshold
The total income required to sustain local livelihoods. This means total expenditure to:
(1) ensure basic survival (ie, all items covered in the **survival threshold**)
(2) maintain access to basic services – for example, health and education
(3) sustain livelihoods in the medium to longer term – for example, purchase of seeds or veterinary drugs
(4) achieve a minimum locally acceptable standard of living – for example, purchase of basic clothing or coffee/tea.

Livelihood zones
Geographical areas within which people share broadly the same patterns of access to food and income, and have the same access to markets.

Outcome analysis
An analysis of how access to food and cash for each **wealth group** will be affected by a defined hazard, and of the extent to which other food or cash sources can be added or expanded, or non-essential expenditure reduced, to make up the initial shortages.

Problem specification
The translation of a **hazard** such as drought into economic consequences at household level.

Projected outcome
A quantified estimate of access to food and cash, taking into account the shock and household responses to it, in relation to a **survival threshold** and **livelihoods protection threshold**.

Proportional piling
A participatory tool used to estimate percentages, where a set number of beans or stones or similar items are divided by community members to represent percentage shares of some item.

Reference period
A defined period (typically 12 months) to which the **baseline** information refers, needed in order to analyse how changes in the future (in production, for example) can be defined in relation to the baseline.

Risk
The likelihood that an event such as drought or flooding will occur.

Scenario outcome
A quantified estimate of access to food and cash arising from an **outcome analysis**, taking into account the effects of the hazard and household responses to it, for each of the **wealth groups**.

Seasonal calendar
A graphical presentation of the months in which food and cash crop production and key food and income acquisition strategies take place, also showing key seasonal periods such as the rains, periods of peak illness and the hunger season.

Survival threshold
The total food and cash income required to cover the food and non-food items necessary for survival in the short term. It includes (1) 100% of minimum food energy needs; (2) the costs associated with food preparation and consumption; and (3) where applicable, the cost of water for human consumption.

Vulnerability
People are vulnerable if they are expected to be unable to cope with a defined **hazard**; for example, they are vulnerable to crop failure if such a hazard is likely to reduce their access to food or cash below a defined threshold.

Wealth breakdown
The process by which people within a **livelihood zone** are grouped together using local definitions of wealth and the quantification of their assets. The level of division depends on how the community view their society, and the purpose of the analysis.

Wealth group
A group of households within the same community who share similar capacities to exploit the different food and income options within a particular **livelihood zone**.

1 Introduction to the guide

1.1 About the toolkit

The Household Economy Approach: A guide for programme planners and policy-makers is part of a toolkit produced by Save the Children and FEG Consulting for the southern Africa Regional Hunger and Vulnerability Programme (RHVP).

The toolkit was developed in order to assist the RHVP in its objective of strengthening the capacity of government and national and international non-governmental organisation (NGO) staff to undertake accurate, reliable and relevant vulnerability assessment and analysis in southern Africa, especially within national Vulnerability Assessment Committees (VACs) and the Southern Africa Development Community Regional VAC (SADC–RVAC). It is hoped that the toolkit will improve the quality of analysis on which response decisions are made and help to identify, design and implement effective measures to address the problems of vulnerability in the region.

Guidance on the Household Economy Approach (HEA) has to date been provided by the manual *The Household Economy Approach – A resource manual for practitioners*, produced by Save the Children in 2000, and by resources and training materials produced since then by FEG and Save the Children. The toolkit aims to bring together and consolidate this considerable volume of material and provide an up-to-date guide to the approach, to its use in the field and to its application for particular purposes.

The toolkit comprises three elements:
1. *The Practitioners' Guide to HEA*: this is a practical 'how to' guide for those participating in the field work and analysis of a household economy assessment, available at savethechildren.org.uk
2. *The Household Economy Approach: A guide for programme planners and policy-makers*: this is targeted primarily at those who are involved in using assessment results to inform decisions on response and to assist in programme planning. It aims to help policy-makers and programme planners understand the methodology, interpret results and engage

critically in the process of translating results into programme and policy recommendations.
3. *The HEA Training Guide*: this is targeted at those facilitating HEA trainings and comprises guidance materials on organising and running a training, including session outlines, exercises and presentations.

1.2 About the guide

The Household Economy Approach: A guide for programme planners and policy-makers aims to provide an overview of the approach and how it is implemented in the field and applied for different purposes. It begins with an overview of the analytical framework (Chapter 2), outlining the essential steps involved in HEA and why they are necessary. Chapter 3 then describes the applications to which HEA has been put over the past 15 years, ranging from its well-tested use in emergency needs assessment to its more recent application in the sphere of poverty reduction and social protection. The guide then gives an overview of how HEA is carried out (Chapter 4) – how information has been collected in the field to date, and the tools that assist in HEA analysis – and considers why such field methods are used and whether the information and analysis is reliable (Chapter 5). The linkages between HEA and other approaches and areas of inquiry are described in Chapter 6, which also outlines how HEA can be applied to a number of issues of relevance in the analysis of vulnerability, poverty and chronic food insecurity. Some of the criticisms that have been made of HEA are discussed in Chapter 7. Finally, a number of the products that can be generated from an HEA analysis are outlined in Chapter 8.

2 What is HEA?

2.1 Why did HEA come about?

HEA arose from a collaboration in the early 1990s between Save the Children and the Global Information and Early Warning System of the Food and Agriculture Organization (FAO) of the United Nations. The aim was to improve FAO's ability to predict short-term changes in a population's access to food. At that time, it was already widely recognised that rural people in poor countries do not depend solely on their own production for survival, but employ a range of usually market-oriented strategies to get the food and cash they need; and that it is therefore people's ability to gain access to enough food, rather than only their ability to produce it themselves, that determines the likelihood of hunger or famine. The growth and acceptance of this idea followed Amartya Sen's theory of exchange entitlements, which suggested that famines occur not from an absolute lack of food but from people's inability to obtain access to that food.[1] But the difficulties in operationalising this concept of 'access' meant that early warning methodologies tended to focus largely on monitoring food supply, using rainfall, production and price data. A form of analysis was needed that could translate an understanding of how people gain access to food and income, and of how that might be affected by a shock, into practical information to guide more effective decision-making.

To be useful, the approach had to be capable not just of indicating that people are failing to obtain enough food, but of quantifying the problem and suggesting possible approaches to intervention. It had to yield results in a common currency that allow comparison between different areas and groups so that resources can be prioritised and goods or services allocated according to need. The approach had to be capable of providing reliable information on large populations with diverse economies, at reasonable cost. And, crucially, it had to be a predictive approach, to allow for the assessment of future need. These requirements directed HEA's development hand-in-hand with the conviction that an understanding of people's normal economy – how they usually make a living, their savings, reserves and assets – had to be at the core of any approach seeking to gauge the impact of shocks on households.

The approach has come a long way since then. The fact that an understanding of livelihoods is at its heart has led to its application beyond famine early warning; the timeline in the Appendix shows the milestones in the development, application and adoption of HEA over the years. It has been used in different settings and for different purposes, and has been refined and adapted in response to both field experience and the needs of particular decision-makers. These needs, while varied in context and scope, in nearly all cases boil down to certain fundamental questions, as relevant to designing an intervention for social protection as to contingency planning for emergencies: Where is assistance needed, and of what type? Who needs it? How much do they need, when and for how long? Table 1 shows how the steps that make up the HEA framework and its characteristics relate directly back to these questions.

Table 1: Methodological requirements in relation to core questions for programme planning

Core question	Methodological requirement
Who?	Need to disaggregate population and to prioritise between groups/areas. A common 'currency' is required.
What?	A basic understanding of normal livelihood assets is needed to determine what is appropriate and how to 'do no harm'.
How much?	Quantification of livelihood assets and strategies is required as well as understanding of effects of shocks.
Where?	Geographic zoning required.
When and for how long?	A predictive model is needed, with the ability to monitor against a baseline.

2.2 What is HEA?

The Household Economy Approach is a livelihoods-based framework for analysing the way people obtain access to the things they need to survive and prosper. It helps determine people's food and income needs and identify appropriate means of assistance, whether short-term emergency interventions or longer-term development programmes or policy changes. It is based on the principle that an understanding of how people usually make ends meet is essential for assessing how livelihoods will be affected by acute or medium-term economic or ecological change and for planning interventions that will support, rather than undermine, their existing survival strategies.

Central to HEA is an analysis of how people in different circumstances get the food and cash they need, of their assets, the opportunities open to them and the constraints they face, and of the options open to them at times of crisis. It involves the analysis of the connections between different groups and between different areas, providing a picture of how assets are distributed within a community and who gets what from whom.

It is important to note here that HEA is an analytical framework, not a method of information collection. It defines the information that needs to be collected and the way in which it should be analysed in order to answer a particular set of questions. Over the past 15 years, the information needed for HEA analysis has been gathered largely through the use of rapid appraisal methods and semi-structured interviewing of focus groups. This is because experience has shown that these methods are an effective and efficient way of gathering and cross-checking the required information, given the time and funding usually allowed. But HEA is a framework that can use data gathered using a broad range of tools, provided that appropriate measures can be taken to ensure data quality. There are aspects of the baseline, such as household size and composition, for example, or spending on healthcare, that would be obtained very effectively through survey methods; for such information, secondary data sources or targeted survey work add tremendous value. Randomly sampled surveys containing demographic information may also be a more flexible way than purposively sampled focus group discussions to disaggregate household economy information below the wealth group level. Other aspects of the framework – such as the monitoring information required to put together the problem specifications, or to track outcome predictions – may also be better suited to household survey

> **HEA is an analytical framework, not a method of information collection. It defines the information that needs to be gathered and the way it should be analysed in order to answer a particular set of questions.**

methods, depending on time, funding and personnel. The use of rapid appraisal methods is dealt with further in Chapter 5, 'Is HEA reliable?'.

The HEA analytical framework

HEA was developed on the principle that information on events that beset a particular area or community – late rains, land reform, rising food prices, falling cotton prices, closure of mines – can only be properly interpreted if seen against the context of how people normally live. For instance, households that depend on their own production for much of their food needs will be affected by crop failure more severely than households that buy more of their food using income gained from casual employment in the towns. These more market-dependent households, however, will be affected to a greater extent by a rise in food prices or by macroeconomic events that undermine employment opportunities. In other words, an understanding of people's livelihoods is essential for analysing the impact of any significant change – including positive change such as programme interventions or policy changes, as well as climate, market or political shocks – on households. The conceptual framework used in HEA is shown in Figure 1.

The first bar in the chart represents total access to food and income in a normal year. This is the **baseline**, which presents a picture of the 'normal' household economy: household assets; the strategies employed to derive food and income and the relationships between households and with the wider economy; and how households use that income to meet their basic needs, for investment or for social obligations.

One important point to make here is that the quantities represented in the bar charts are a percentage of minimum food energy requirements. In other words, all food and income sources have been converted into their calorie equivalencies and then compared with the internationally accepted standard of 2,100 kilocalories (kcals) per person per day. This has the advantage of allowing for like-with-like comparisons, and also of ensuring that a rigorous cross-checking can take place. In most instances, HEA uses the measure of 2,100 kilocalories rather than a more sophisticated nutritional measure (such as the ideal dietary composition) because this meets the immediate requirements of the decision-makers who tend to demand HEA information, and it fits within the practical limitations of most assessments. This is not to say that energy alone is a sufficient measure of nutritional adequacy; but it is the first measure of whether or not people will starve. Further analysis along

2 WHAT IS HEA?

Figure 1: The HEA analytical framework – a simplified illustration

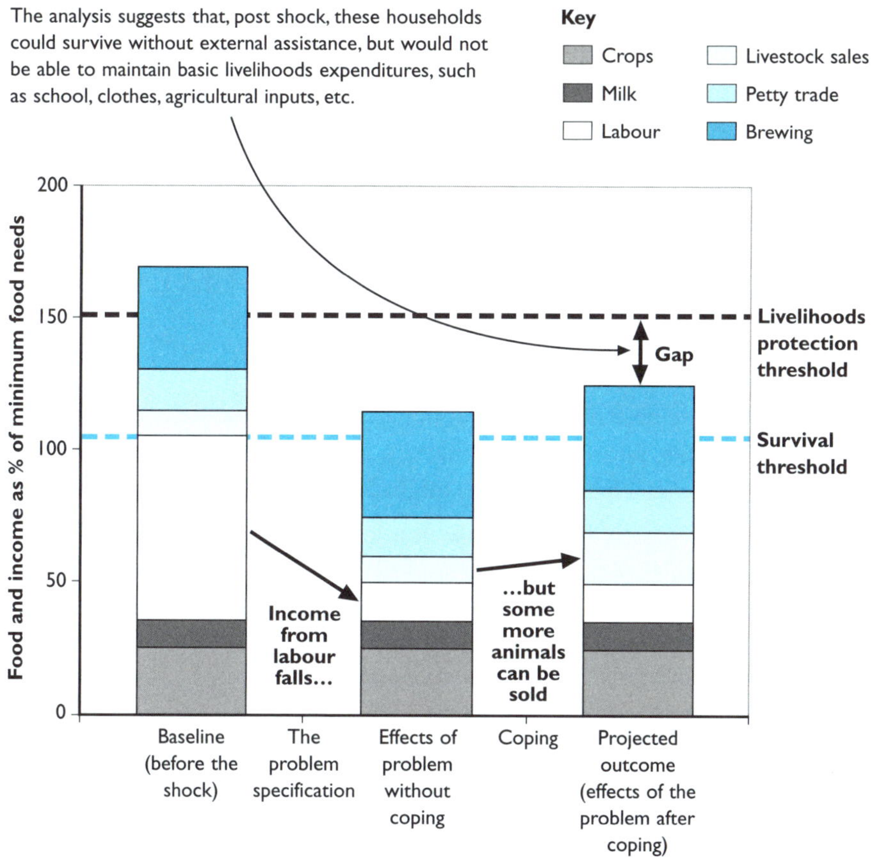

The analysis suggests that, post shock, these households could survive without external assistance, but would not be able to maintain basic livelihoods expenditures, such as school, clothes, agricultural inputs, etc.

Key
- Crops
- Milk
- Labour
- Livestock sales
- Petty trade
- Brewing

Food and income as % of minimum food needs

- Livelihoods protection threshold
- Gap
- Survival threshold

Income from labour falls…

…but some more animals can be sold

- Baseline (before the shock)
- The problem specification
- Effects of problem without coping
- Coping
- Projected outcome (effects of the problem after coping)

Baseline: The first bar shows total access to food and income in a normal year. This is the baseline picture before the shock.

Effects of problem without coping: The second bar shows how access is affected by a shock like the closure of commercial farms. In this case, labour opportunities by which this household obtains much of its income are cut off.

Projected outcome: The third bar shows access to food and income taking into account the household's coping strategies. In this case, more animals are sold than usual.

The 'y' axis represents food and income as a **percentage of minimum annual food energy needs**. In short, food and income sources have been converted into kilocalories which are then compared to 2100 kcal, which represents the internationally accepted minimum energy requirement per person per day. While simplified in this graphic for the purposes of illustration, this is an important concept in HEA because converting food and income into a common currency allows analysts to quantify and make comparisons.

nutritional lines is possible with HEA, although targeted nutritional survey work is likely to be more appropriate for gaining specific pieces of information. See section 6.2 for more on the relationship between HEA and nutrition.

The second bar in the chart – **the effects of the problem without coping** – shows us how specific sources of food and cash income are affected by a shock. In this case, the shock is the closure of commercial farms, which results in the curtailment of employment opportunities. The effects of shocks are specific to different livelihoods and to different levels of wealth, and the specific problem created by a 'shock' for particular households is defined in HEA as the 'problem specification'. In Figure 1, the problem is shown between bars one and two, and results in reduced income from employment, as shown in bar two.

It is worth noting here that HEA can be used to consider the effects not just of negative shocks, but of positive changes. So, for instance, it is possible to consider just how much extra income might be obtained by poorer households that are provided with two goats, and what this might mean in terms of increased food security. Or the relative food security benefits of a subsidy on kerosene might be weighed up against a price cap on staple maize. Throughout this guide, it is important to keep in mind that the term 'shock' is used as a shorthand for any measurable meaningful change that can be modelled, and covers both negative hazards and positive changes.

The framework takes into account household capacity to adapt to the economic stress caused by the hazard by drawing down on assets, cutting down on certain expenditures or expanding other sources of food or cash. This is shown in the **coping** step, which is placed in between the second and third bars above. In this example, households are able to sell more livestock than usual, and this increases their access to food and income. In other cases, it might be that households could find alternative employment opportunities elsewhere, although they would be competing with people in the same position. They might be able to draw further on the social obligations of relatives. Or they might be able to cut down on non-essential expenditure and use the cash for staple food instead.

The final result – the **projected outcome** – is shown in the third bar. The projected outcome is, in essence, a consideration of the extent to which households will be able to (1) meet their basic survival needs (the 'survival threshold') and (2) protect their livelihoods (the 'livelihoods protection threshold'). These thresholds are illustrated in Figure 1 by the two horizontal lines and are described more fully in Figure 7. Decisions about the need for intervention, for what and on what scale, are guided by the baseline data, which encapsulates a knowledge of local livelihoods and coping strategies.

2.3 The steps of the HEA framework

In HEA, the conceptual framework of:

Baseline + Hazard + Response = Outcome

is translated into six steps. These steps, and the rationale behind each of them, are shown in Figure 2. When the analysis shown is conducted for all or most of the livelihood zones within a country, the outcome is a **comparative analysis** of predicted need across the whole country.

At the heart of HEA is a depiction of how people get by from year to year and the connections with other people and places that enable them to do so. This is called the **baseline** and has three components: **livelihood zoning**, a **wealth breakdown** and an **analysis of livelihood strategies** for each of the identified wealth groups.

The **outcome analysis** is the investigation of how that baseline access to food and income might change as a result of a specific hazard, such as drought. It consists of three steps: first, the translation of a hazard such as drought into economic consequences at household level (such as a percentage fall in crop production or increase in food prices compared with the baseline), which is referred to in HEA as the **problem specification**; second, the analysis of the capacity of households in different wealth groups to cope with the hazard themselves (**analysis of coping capacity**); and finally, predicted access to food and income at household level for a defined future period is compared to two thresholds: the survival and livelihood protection thresholds. This last step is referred to as the **projected outcome**.

The same framework can be applied to assessing the impact of a positive change, such as a programme or beneficial price policy. Just as a hazard is translated into its effects on food and income sources (the problem specification), so an intervention can be translated into its possible effects on sources of food and income, expenditure, and asset ownership. Projected access to food and income can be compared both with previous levels and with thresholds defined by criteria such as households' ability to buy livestock or to afford the costs of education.

Figure 2: The six steps of the HEA framework

HEA baseline				HEA outcome analysis		
Step 1: Livelihood zoning →	**Step 2: Wealth breakdown** →	**Step 3: Livelihoods strategies**	+	**Step 4: Problem specification** +	**Step 5: Analysis of coping capacity** =	**Step 6: Projected outcome**
What is it? The delineation of areas within which people share broadly the same patterns of livelihood.	*What is it?* The grouping together of people using local definitions of wealth and the quantification of their assets.	*What is it?* The quantification of sources of food and income, and expenditure patterns, for households in each wealth group.		*What is it?* The translation of a shock (e.g. drought) or an intervention or policy into economic consequences at household level.	*What is it?* An analysis of the capacity of households to respond to the shock.	*What is it?* A quantified estimate of access to food and cash, taking into account the shock and household responses to it, in relation to a survival and livelihoods protection threshold.
Why is it needed? To provide a livelihoods-based sampling frame; to allow you to target assistance geographically; to customise indicators for livelihoods monitoring systems.	*Why is it needed?* To disaggregate the population according to shared patterns of access; to help indicate who needs assistance and how many of them there are.	*Why is it needed?* To provide a quantified estimate of food and income needs and to enable comparisons to be made between wealth groups and livelihood zones.		*Why is it needed?* To enable an analysis of the effects of a shock or change at household level.	*Why is it needed?* To assess how far households can cope on their own without resorting to damaging coping strategies.	*Why is it needed?* For planning relief or service provision, contingency planning, or modelling the possible effects of proposed interventions.

Each of the steps is outlined below.

2.4 The baseline: steps 1 to 3

Grouping households together in some way is necessary in any population analysis, since it is not possible to consider each household individually; the most logical way of doing this for the purposes of livelihood analysis is to group people who share similar livelihoods – that is, similar patterns of access to food and income. How people gain access to food and income is determined by two main factors: geography (since this determines what the options are) and wealth (since this determines how people can utilise those options). The first two steps in an HEA assessment are, therefore, livelihood zoning and the identification of wealth groups.

Step 1: Livelihood zoning

People's options for obtaining food and cash income are determined to a great extent by where they live. In Swaziland, for example, households in the dry lowveld region where the agro-ecology is suited more to herding will have very different options from those in the wetter mid- and highveld areas, which favour agriculture. But it is not just agro-ecology which determines livelihood patterns – it is access to markets. Market access affects both the ability of people to sell their production (crops or livestock or other items) and the price they obtain for these goods. In addition, there are labour 'markets' – centres of demand for casual or salaried workers. Thus, households with good access to the urban complex of Manzini, Mbabane and Matsapha in Swaziland have different options from those living in the western mountains.

A livelihood zone is an area within which people share basically the same patterns of access to food (that is, they grow the same crops, or keep the same types of livestock), and have the same access to markets. An example of a livelihood zone map from Mozambique is given in Figure 3 (overleaf). This shows how the zoning takes into account differences not just in production but in access to employment markets (which distinguishes livelihoods in the Lower Limpopo from those in the Upper Limpopo), and access to trading markets (which is the distinguishing feature of livelihoods in the coastal zone).

Zoning involves the preparation of maps, together with analyses of the options for obtaining food and income within each zone and the marketing networks that determine the patterns of exchange between zones. Taken together, the

• THE HOUSEHOLD ECONOMY APPROACH

Figure 3: Example of a livelihood zone map: the Limpopo Basin, Mozambique

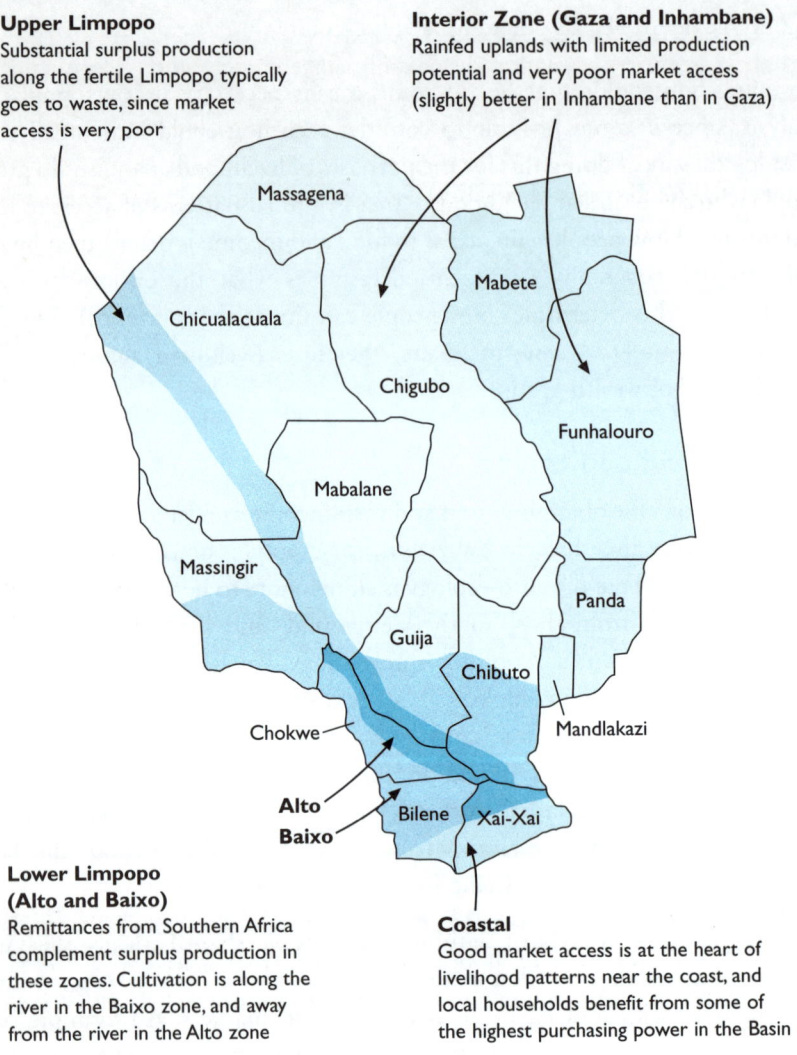

Upper Limpopo
Substantial surplus production along the fertile Limpopo typically goes to waste, since market access is very poor

Interior Zone (Gaza and Inhambane)
Rainfed uplands with limited production potential and very poor market access (slightly better in Inhambane than in Gaza)

Lower Limpopo (Alto and Baixo)
Remittances from Southern Africa complement surplus production in these zones. Cultivation is along the river in the Baixo zone, and away from the river in the Alto zone

Coastal
Good market access is at the heart of livelihood patterns near the coast, and local households benefit from some of the highest purchasing power in the Basin

Livelihood zones are delineated on the basis of differences in production and in access to markets.

In the Limpopo Basin, production is high all along the river, but livelihoods are by no means homogeneous.

Those nearer the coast and in the lower reaches of the Limpopo benefit respectively from good access to markets for selling produce and from good access to the South African employment market.

three factors of geography, production system, and the marketing system by and large determine the economic operations of households within a particular livelihood zone. They also determine vulnerability to particular hazards such as drought, insecurity, or market dislocation, since vulnerability is a function of the normal activities of households and of the activities they turn to in response to a hazard.

But are livelihood zones of practical use, given that they do not always follow administrative boundaries?

Livelihood zones and administrative divisions

It is quite common to find different patterns of livelihood within one district, and certainly within one region. In Swaziland, for instance, all four administrative regions contain parts of several different livelihood zones, reflecting lowveld versus middleveld ecologies.

However, decisions on resource allocation and service provision are made on the basis of administrative areas and units, so HEA livelihood zones tend to be aligned as far as possible with lower-level administrative or customary boundaries. In Malawi they have been lined up with Extension Planning Area (EPA) boundaries; in Swaziland with chiefdom boundaries. This way, populations in the livelihood zones can be identified and responded to along administrative lines, and a more disaggregated analysis can be carried out using data relating to lower-level administrative divisions, where it is available.

Step 2: Wealth breakdown

While geography tends to define a household's options for obtaining food and income, the ability to exploit those options and to survive in a crisis is determined largely by wealth. In other words, what people have by way of land, capital and livestock, together with their educational status and access to political and social networks, determines the ways in which they will be able to get food and cash, or how they will respond to sudden or long-term change. Poor households with little land may work for better-off households to get money to buy food; the better-off may use profits from agriculture as capital to engage in trade. Wealth may also affect households' exposure to a hazard, especially in conflict situations where those with greater wealth may become targets for attack. In the event of a crisis, poor and better-off households will be affected differently and, therefore, warrant separate examination. The

• THE HOUSEHOLD ECONOMY APPROACH

Figure 4: Example of a wealth breakdown: Chongwe-Nyimba Plateau Valley Livelihood Zone, Zambia

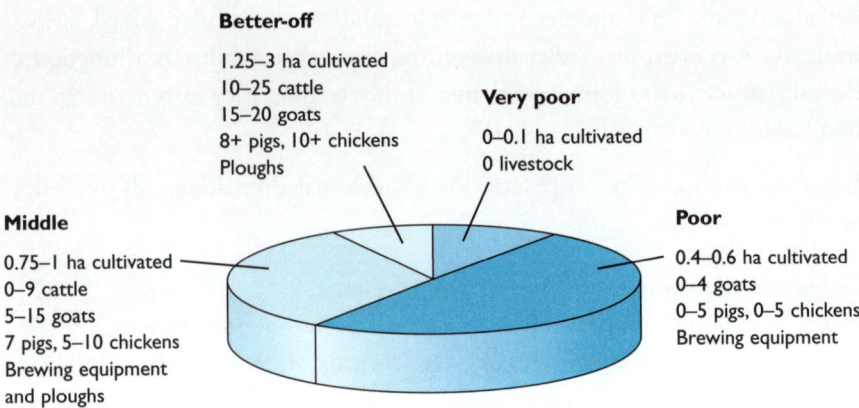

Better-off
1.25–3 ha cultivated
10–25 cattle
15–20 goats
8+ pigs, 10+ chickens
Ploughs

Very poor
0–0.1 ha cultivated
0 livestock

Middle
0.75–1 ha cultivated
0–9 cattle
5–15 goats
7 pigs, 5–10 chickens
Brewing equipment
and ploughs

Poor
0.4–0.6 ha cultivated
0–4 goats
0–5 pigs, 0–5 chickens
Brewing equipment

The main determinant of wealth in this livelihood zone is cattle ownership, which in turn determines the number of plough oxen that a household owns and the area of land that they are able to cultivate. The number of other types of livestock owned and the agricultural inputs that a household can afford are also related to this.

The **very poor** group includes households that are headed by elderly, terminally ill or widowed members, often supporting small numbers of young dependants, some of whom may be orphaned by AIDS. Households in this group are highly dependent on gifts and handouts. The poor are highly dependent on the labour opportunities provided by the middle and better-off groups.

Source: Zambia Vulnerability Assessment Committee (2004)

investigation of differences between households is central to an analysis of food security and vulnerability to different hazards.

To capture these variations, HEA seeks to characterise typical households within each zone according to at least three (commonly four and sometimes more) wealth groups. In the field, wealth categories are defined through interviews with community key informants. 'Poor' and 'better-off' are thus relative to local rather than external standards. Often, these standards are predictable along general livelihood lines: landholding size, labour availability and draught power define wealth in a poor agricultural economy; land quality and access to fishing equipment in agro-fishing communities; the size of herds in pastoral economies. Family size – specifically the balance between young and mature children – is often a factor in wealth definitions.

But what if a programme planner seeks to support groups of people defined in demographic or administrative terms, such as female-headed households, pensioners or households supporting HIV/AIDS orphans? Where such population groups share a common pattern of livelihood, they can be analysed in the usual way; in Serbia, HEA analyses have been carried out on groups of pensioner households (see section 3.2), and in Macedonia on 'social cases', which included those physically unable to work, low-income pensioners, the low-income unemployed and single mothers (see section 3.5). Where there is more variation in livelihood patterns within these groups, and/or where more flexibility is required in the analysis, HEA can take a more disaggregated approach (see section 4.3).

> **HEA wealth breakdowns focus on what causes difference in wealth (such as access to land, labour and capital).**
>
> **This is distinct from a 'wealth ranking', which focuses on indicators, or outcomes, of wealth, such as roofing type or number of assets.**

Finally, wealth breakdowns allow us to look at the connections between different wealth groups. The rich and poor within a community are almost always connected in some way; commonly, the poor are dependent on the rich for casual agricultural employment, or for gifts or loans of food or cash. Sometimes, the poor take care of some of the livestock of the better-off, benefiting from the milk or keeping part of the progeny of smallstock as the reward – the only means by which they can accumulate assets themselves. Such connections need to be taken into account both for understanding how the poor survive in normal and bad years, and for identifying effective poverty reduction measures.

> **In southern Africa, the poor are commonly dependent on the rich for casual agricultural employment. This provides the poor with an important source of income. But it makes them vulnerable to any decline in expenditure on the part of the rich – for example, as a result of HIV/AIDS.**

Step 3: Analysis of livelihood strategies

Having grouped households according to where they live and their wealth, the next step is to examine patterns of food and cash income and patterns of expenditure over a defined reference period. This gives a baseline picture of exactly how households get the food they eat and the cash they need, and how they spend their money. These are the three pillars of HEA analysis.

Quantification of food, income and expenditure

Many approaches to livelihood analysis describe how people acquire food and cash. The difference with HEA is that it provides quantitative information; information is gathered on how much food or cash households gain from a particular source, and on how much they spend on certain items and basic services over the defined period. Figure 5 gives an example of such a data set and some of the observations that can be drawn from it.

As well as providing an acute perspective on household operations and constraints, quantification is needed to allow a new situation – say, the loss of employment opportunities or poor rains – to be judged in terms of its likely effect on livelihoods. It allows decision-makers to compare levels of need across different populations and areas, and to prioritise and allocate resources accordingly. The need to compare and prioritise applies as much to decisions on tackling chronic poverty (which groups are the poorest, and where are they?) as it does to emergency resource allocation. Equally, a quantified approach is needed for assessing and comparing the impact of positive change on different groups and different areas.

That is not to say that the information gained consists of figures alone or that it lacks the capacity to provide a 'qualitative' analysis of the conditions and situation of the households studied. HEA is a systems-based, rather than a correlative, approach. This means that conclusions are drawn from a holistic analysis of livelihoods – that is, taking into account all the means

> **HEA is a systems-based, rather than a correlative approach. It does not seek to find relationships between selected indicators but rather aims to build up a holistic picture of livelihoods. This means that each piece of information gathered has to make sense in relation to the rest.**

2 WHAT IS HEA?

Figure 5: Baseline data from West Zambezi Livelihood Zone, Zambia

Sources of food

Poor households get less than half of their food from their fields. Half of the balance comes from working for others and being paid directly in staple food. The other half comes from market purchase or bartering fish, from direct fish catch consumption, from the collection of seasonal wild foods and from relief. All these activities give them less than 100% of their basic food requirement. This is the structure of food insecurity.

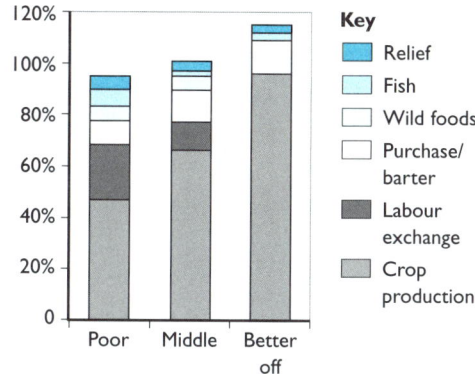

Key: Relief, Fish, Wild foods, Purchase/barter, Labour exchange, Crop production

Sources of cash

We also see the constraints of poverty: the poor cannot afford to buy the grain and other inputs to do brewing, one of the main income sources of the middle group. The proportionately biggest earner is livestock, which the poor have virtually none to sell, and they have no cash crops either. They cannot even afford the hives that allow profitable honey production.

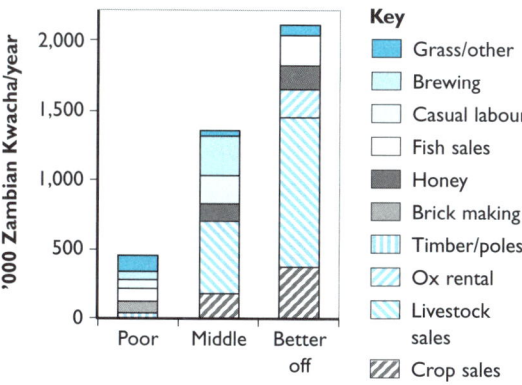

Key: Grass/other, Brewing, Casual labour, Fish sales, Honey, Brick making, Timber/poles, Ox rental, Livestock sales, Crop sales

Patterns of expenditure

As to quality of life, the poor have exceedingly little to spend on other food like relish, or on almost anything else.

And what of the chronic nature of poverty? The poor – and even the middle, who are pretty poor too – have very little to spend on agricultural inputs, so they can't improve their own production. They have very little to spend on education (the main component of social services) so that secondary school especially, which can offer a future, is beyond the means of perhaps half the population.

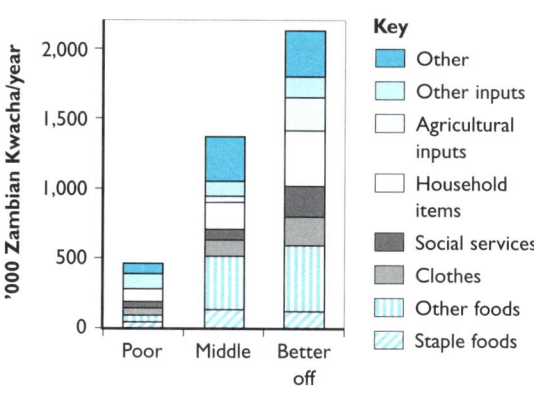

Key: Other, Other inputs, Agricultural inputs, Household items, Social services, Clothes, Other foods, Staple foods

Source: Zambia Vulnerability Assessment Committee (2004)

by which people survive, all their resources and all their options – rather than from an analysis that aims to find relationships between selected factors or symptoms such as prices and rates of migration or of wild food collection. The aim of the baseline inquiry is, therefore, to build up a logical and comprehensive picture of livelihoods that is amenable to such a systems analysis, and each 'bit' of information gathered has to make sense in relation to the rest. In these terms the approach gains rigour from the fact that the information has to 'add up' in quantitative, as well as logical, terms.

This holistic view of livelihoods also has implications for the internal consistency of the information gathered. The way in which HEA information is usually collected is described in Chapter 4, 'How is HEA done?', and the question of the reliability of the information is considered in Chapter 5, 'Is HEA reliable?'. But it is worth noting here that the nature of the information sought in an HEA inquiry makes it possible to check for consistency. There are two sides to the equation that must match. On one side, there is a finite and relatively small number of economic options available to households; these define the broad parameters of the investigation. On the other, there is a minimum food energy requirement that households must be at least close to meeting if they are surviving, and a certain level of income they have to acquire in order to afford their stated expenditure. By comparing the two sides of the equations, and through a number of other cross-checks, gaps and inconsistencies in the information can be challenged and a coherent and logical account of how households make ends meet can be put together. See section 5.4 for more on cross-checking in HEA.

Seasonality

Among the rural poor, seasonal variations in food access, on-farm labour requirements and employment opportunities tend to define the livelihood options that people pursue and the constraints they face. This has implications for the timing of both emergency and longer-term interventions. A seasonal analysis of food and income acquisition strategies (see Figure 6 for an example) is therefore a key part of the baseline analysis. A seasonal or month-by-month HEA analysis can also bring to light the extremely tight financial margins by which the poor survive (see the example of poor, female-headed households in Ethiopia in section 3.4).

2 WHAT IS HEA?

Figure 6: Seasonal calendar – West Zambezi LZ, Zambia

		Sep	Oct	Nov	Dec	Jan	Feb	Mar	Apr	May	Jun	Jul	Aug
Crop production	Land preparation												
	Planting												
	Weeding												
	Green harvest												
	Cassava harvest												
	Rice harvest												
	Maize harvest												
	Sorghum harvest												
	Millet harvest												
Other income	Fishing												
	Wild food collection												
	Casual labour												
Maize price peak													
Flooding peak													
Hunger season													
Rainfall pattern													
		Sep	Oct	Nov	Dec	Jan	Feb	Mar	Apr	May	Jun	Jul	Aug

Source: Zambia Vulnerability Assessment Committee (2004)

Markets

Most households in most parts of the world depend on the marketplace to buy some or all of their basic needs and to earn the cash with which to do so. Understanding the links between communities and their different markets allows us to assess their options in times of crisis. HEA assessments examine where people buy different goods, where those goods come from, where people sell the goods and services they themselves supply and where they go or come from to look for work. We need to know how commodity prices and labour rates change from season to season and how this corresponds with the need of (particularly poor) households to buy or sell or work. We need to know which markets are of greatest importance in order to judge how changes in price or access to particular markets will affect households over a wider geography. The links between HEA and market analysis are described further in section 6.2.

Use of baselines

Once the baselines have been compiled, they can be used repeatedly over a number of years until significant changes in the underlying economy render them invalid. Rural economies in developing countries tend not to change rapidly, and a good baseline will generally be valid for between five and ten years. What varies is the prevailing level of food security, but this is a function of variations in hazard, not variations in the baseline. Put another way, the level of maize production may vary from year to year (hazard), but the underlying pattern of agricultural production does not (the baseline).

Any event that causes fundamental change in the household economy, such as the introduction of irrigation, or a construction boom, will require the updating of a baseline, but such changes should be distinguished from the inevitable fluctuations in asset ownership that arise as a result of good and bad years. These also need to be taken into account, but can be tracked through monitoring and wealth breakdown exercises and entered into the analysis as part of the problem specification.

The picture of household economy that is built up in this way can in itself be put to a number of uses, as described in Chapter 2, 'How has HEA been used?'. In outline:
1. It provides the starting point for analysing vulnerability, helping to identify the particular risks to which groups are vulnerable and therefore the circumstances in which they are likely to experience food insecurity in the future (see section 3.3).
2. It gives us a framework by which we can analyse the effect of specific shocks, such as a drought or rapid price inflation (see sections 3.2 and 3.3).
3. It enables us to identify possible options for interventions to address chronic poverty. It does this by:
    - helping to distinguish chronic livelihood insecurity problems that exist in a 'normal' year from more acute problems that occur as a result of shocks (see section 6.3)

- helping to determine levels of poverty by comparing income levels for different groups with the cost of a 'minimum non-food basket', together with the cost of food purchase, to see whether households can access basic needs (see sections 3.1 and 6.3)
- helping to identify possible options for supporting the economic development of the poor, through an analysis of constraints and opportunities (see sections 3.4 and 3.6).

4. It provides a framework for modelling the possible impact of an intervention on the household economy (see section 3.5).

Once the baseline is established, an analysis can be carried out of the likely impact of a shock or hazard in a bad year. This is called the outcome analysis.

2.5 Outcome analysis: steps 4 to 6

As a predictive approach, HEA is concerned with assessing the effect that a particular shock or change will have on household access to food and income. This is done by assessing (1) how baseline access to food and cash will be affected by the shock or change; and (2) the extent to which households will be able to make up the initial shortages through various coping strategies or, in the case of positive change, the contribution any additional or freed-up income would make to the household economy.

The effectiveness of an early warning tool clearly hinges on its ability to predict; contingency plans need to be built on the basis of scenarios that show what is likely to happen over the coming six to 12 months. But a predictive facility is also important because agencies need to plan for service provision or deliveries for the time at which they are likely to arrive. A needs assessment approach is of little use (and is potentially even harmful) if it only assesses current needs, and does not allow agencies to plan according to a realistic implementation timetable. For example, by the time emergency or rehabilitation aid has reached people (with typical lead times of up to six months required), it may be unnecessary at best, and in the worst cases harmful.

The ability to predict how livelihoods will be affected by change is also essential in considering the possible impact at household level of poverty reduction measures. This applies as much to wider policy interventions, such as grain price stabilisation, as it does to transfers targeted at households.

• THE HOUSEHOLD ECONOMY APPROACH

Step 4: Analysis of hazard and problem specification

The first step in analysing how the baseline household economy will be affected by a particular hazard is to analyse the hazard itself. Just knowing that a hazard might occur or has occurred is not sufficient for the analytical purposes of HEA. The hazard must be translated into quantified economic consequences that link clearly to baseline information on livelihood strategies.

For example, production failure in southern Africa can have a number of consequences in relation to agricultural livelihoods beyond the obvious loss of crop and livestock production. These consequences include the loss of income from local agricultural employment, from cash crop sales and from livestock sales (through reduced prices), and the reduced availability of wild foods.

> In order to be able to analyse the full impact of a hazard on livelihoods, it has to be translated into economic consequences that link to the baseline information on food and income sources.

In compiling the hazard information, the first thing to do is to determine the relevant shock factors for analysis, using the baseline information as a guide. For each wealth group and livelihood zone, it is important to identify those sources of food or cash that contribute significantly to total food or cash income because a reduction in access to that one source may have a significant effect on total access. That income source can then be monitored and the current year compared with the reference year. In most cases crop production and price information will be essential information to analyse. However, there may be cases, for instance, with fishing communities or pastoralist groups, where crop production is of minimal importance.

Information on natural hazards, such as crop and pasture failure, is obtained from existing crop or market price monitoring systems and seasonal or annual field assessments. Information on shocks arising from economic or political events, such as land reform or inflation, is obtained from a political and economic analysis of events and future trends, which can show how prices will change, what markets will do or which state entitlements will be lost. In both cases, hazard information needs to be broken down into its effects on households' sources of food and income, expressed as a percentage of the baseline. This is called the problem specification. An example from the Malawi food security assessment of 2004 is shown in Table 2. How the hazards of drought and land reform might be broken down in this way is shown in Table 3 overleaf.

Table 2: Problem specification for Thyolo and Mulanje Livelihood Zone, Malawi 2004

Assumptions for this projection	% of baseline
Crop production (based upon RDP-level information)*	
Maize	50%
Rice	70%
Sweet potatoes	45%
Cassava	50%
Pulses	20%
Bananas	70%
Fruits/vegetables	90%
Other crops	100%
Tobacco sales price[†]	100%
Ganyu	
Availability	75%
Payment	100%
Self employment[†]	50%
Other sources of food and income	100%
Scenario 1 market purchase price for maize[†]	20 MK/kg
Scenario 2 market purchase price for maize[†]	26 MK/kg
Cost of basic non-food items[†]	120%[2]
Other prices[†]	100%

*Baseline = average production 1998–2002
[†] Baseline = average price 2002–03 marketing year

Source: Malawi NVAC (2004)[2]

Table 3: Translation of production and macroeconomic hazards into problem specifications

Macro-level shock	Natural hazard			Man-made hazard		
	Drought			Land reform		
Impact at meso-level	Reduction in crop production	Reduction in livestock production	Reduced availability of wild foods	Commercial farm workers laid off	Farmers re-settled but with insufficient inputs to take full advantage of allocated land	Reduced domestic grain production
Effect at household level (problem specification)	Loss of food from own crops • Loss of income from crop sales • Increase in grain prices • Loss of local on-farm employment	Loss in milk yields and availability • Decline in livestock prices	Loss of food from wild foods	Loss of formal farming income for commercial farm workers	Decline in availability of agricultural employment for seasonal migrants • Decline in agricultural labour wage rates	Increase in grain prices

The task of obtaining the information necessary to create a 'problem specification' is clearly important, but one which HEA is not designed to undertake. HEA relies on meteorological and agricultural systems to provide predictions of crop production or pasture availability. Similarly, it relies on others to do the political and economic analysis required to predict future trends. HEA takes up the reins at the point where these analyses leave off, determining how these macro-level changes will affect specific food and cash-income sources at the household level. Where analysis at the macro-level does not exist or is of poor quality, HEA practitioners may at least, working with a broad view of the economic or political situation and an understanding of what households are vulnerable to, be able to ask some of the right questions to determine the nature and scale of future shocks. The focus group discussions and semi-structured interviews commonly used in HEA make it amenable to incorporating inquiry at this level, provided that additional interviewing time is budgeted.

The translation of hazards into problem specifications is an important point of connection between HEA and other information and analytical systems, and an area in which collaboration tends to be fruitful.

Step 5: Analysis of coping capacity

This step takes account of the response strategies that different types of household will employ to try to deal with the problems they face. The key questions are:
- Which of the existing food and income options can be expanded in current circumstances?
- What additional options can be pursued?
- Can expenditure be reduced?
- What effect will these responses have on access to food (ie, *how much* extra food can be obtained in these ways)?

In other words, this is a quantified analysis of households' ability to diversify and expand access to various sources of food and income, and thus to cope with a specified hazard. Information on the options open to households when a problem strikes is collected during the baseline study, usually by referring back to previous years and investigating the extent to which particular sources of food or cash could be expanded.

As in the case of the baseline analysis, the analysis of household coping capacity provides insights into the opportunities for, and constraints in, expanding food and income options in different areas, highlighting where and how the various options might be supported by different types of intervention.

Not every response strategy available to households is included in an outcome analysis. Strategies may be excluded if they have undesirable or damaging side effects that threaten the sustainability of livelihoods in the medium to longer term, such as selling all productive assets, taking children out of school or entering into prostitution. The aim of assistance may not only be to prevent outright hunger, but to minimise the use of damaging response strategies, preserve assets and protect livelihoods. HEA enables various levels of intervention to be modelled that explicitly either include or exclude particular coping strategies (see, for example, the Serbia scenario analysis in section 3.2).

> Particular household response strategies may be excluded from the outcome analysis if they have undesirable or damaging side effects.

Thus, only those strategies that are appropriate responses to local stress are included. In this context, 'appropriate' means both 'considered a normal response by the local population' and 'unlikely to damage local livelihoods in the medium to longer term'. In many agricultural areas, for example, it may be usual for one or more household members to migrate for labour when times are hard. Provided the response is not pushed too far (ie, too many people migrating for too long a period of time), this can be considered an appropriate response to stress. Similarly, in a pastoral setting, it is usual to increase livestock sales in a bad year. This again is an appropriate response – provided the increase in sales is not excessive.

In household economy analysis, therefore, the most important characteristic of a response or coping strategy is its cost, where cost is measured in terms of the effect on livelihood assets, on future production by the household, and on the health and welfare of individual household members. But it is important to note that including a particular coping strategy in the analysis does not imply that households will necessarily follow that strategy. For example, if the analysis takes into account the income that could be earned from the sale of additional livestock, it does not imply that households will necessarily take up that strategy. They may decide instead to employ one or more of the other strategies open to them, including those considered to be damaging in some way; they may reduce food intake, or send a household member away permanently to find work. The point is that the analysis of household response is not an attempt to model behaviour – that is, to predict which options households will definitely take up in a crisis and which they won't. Rather, it is an attempt to define a level of access below which households have little choice but to pursue strategies that are likely to be damaging in the long term; in other words, a level of access below which the analysis shows that intervention is appropriate.

> **The objective of the outcome analysis is not to model household behaviour, but to measure access against a threshold below which households will have to pursue damaging coping strategies – and therefore below which intervention is appropriate.**

Step 6: Projected outcome

The output from an outcome analysis is the projected outcome: an estimate of total food and cash income for the current year, once the cumulative effects of current hazards and income generated from coping strategies have been taken into account. To determine whether an intervention of some kind is required, projected total income is then compared against two locally defined thresholds: one defining the minimum survival requirements, and the other setting out what it takes to protect people's livelihoods (see Figure 7 overleaf).

Where HEA is used across a whole country, the analyses of affected livelihood zones together provide a national-level, comparative picture of how different groups and areas are affected and why, and of which interventions may be most appropriate.

Once the projected outcome has been calculated, the core assumptions underlying it need to be monitored. This is critical in ensuring that response plans can be adjusted, either because trends in (for example) prices or employment are diverging from initial assumptions, or because more accurate data (for example, on production) becomes available. Food security monitoring is also important for verifying initial predictions and the

• THE HOUSEHOLD ECONOMY APPROACH

Figure 7: Livelihoods protection and survival thresholds

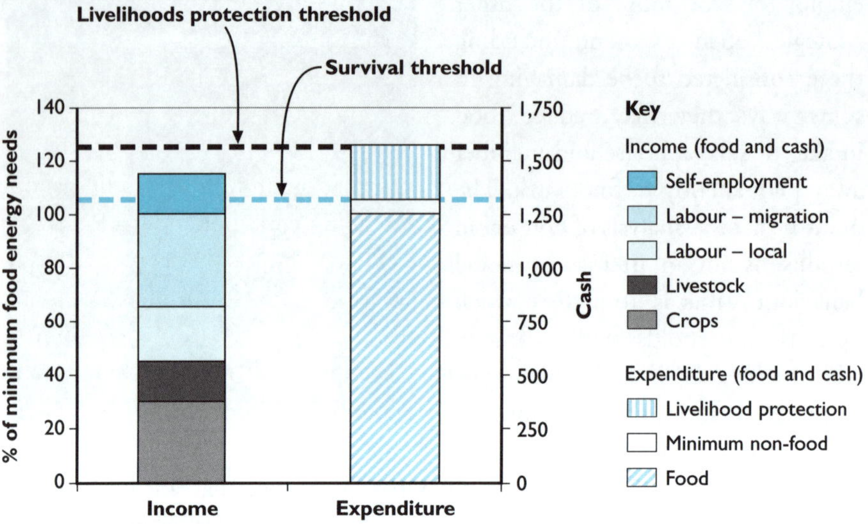

In this example, income is sufficient to cover basic survival needs, but not enough to cover minimum livelihood requirements.

The **survival threshold** represents the total food and cash income required to cover:
a) 100% of minimum food energy needs (2,100 kcals per person), plus
b) the costs associated with food preparation and consumption (ie, salt, soap, kerosene and/or firewood for cooking and basic lighting), plus
c) any expenditure on water for human consumption.
Note: Items included in categories b) and c) together make up the minimum non-food expenditure basket, represented by the white bar in the expenditure graphic.

The **livelihoods protection threshold** represents the total income required to sustain local livelihoods. This means total expenditure to:
a) ensure basic survival (see above), plus
b) maintain access to basic services (eg, routine medical and schooling expenses), plus
c) sustain livelihoods in the medium to longer term (eg, regular purchases of seeds, fertilizer, veterinary drugs, etc), plus
d) achieve a minimum locally acceptable standard of living (eg, purchase of basic clothing, coffee/tea, etc)

effectiveness of response programmes; in the latter half of 2005, for example, data from the Malawi Integrated Nutrition and Food Security Surveillance System (Ministry of Health/Action Against Hunger) played an important role in verifying the initial Malawi Vulnerability Assessment Committee prediction and indicating that the response was far from adequate.[3]

3 How has HEA been used?

HEA has proved to be a rich source of information and understanding about how the poor live. The holistic view of household operations and strategies that it offers is essential for understanding the effect of shocks on people's access to food and cash income; but it is also required as the basis for identifying and planning poverty reduction interventions. Governments and development agencies in southern Africa increasingly recognise the need for longer-term approaches to reducing poor people's vulnerability to shocks. RHVP highlights "the increasing prevalence of chronic vulnerability which is not being effectively addressed by orthodox humanitarian responses… [RHVP] seeks to shift the emphasis of policy from ad hoc emergency responses (primarily food aid) to regular, guaranteed and appropriate social protection measures to meet chronic needs."[4] HEA's quantified household perspective and ability to model impact has proved to be of value in the identification and design of such measures.

Since its inception, the wide range of settings in which HEA has been applied, shown in Table 4 (overleaf), has enabled the approach to be tested in different contexts, for different purposes and for different stages of the project cycle. This chapter outlines how HEA has been used in each case and illustrates each application with an example. We begin with HEA's best-known applications in the **broad 'emergency' sphere**, ranging between early warning of the impact of hazards, predicting future needs under different scenarios, determining current emergency needs and identifying post-recovery support. We then move on to its increasing application in the **poverty reduction and social protection sphere**, from broad guidance on development opportunities and strategies, to determining appropriate safety net transfer levels, quantifying the likely impact of other social protection measures, examining the impact of market interventions and using livelihood interventions to improve access to health and education. The chapter finishes with a review of how HEA can be used later in the project cycle to **monitor and evaluate the impact** of interventions. Examples of the various uses to which HEA has been put are summarised in Table 5 (overleaf).

• THE HOUSEHOLD ECONOMY APPROACH

Table 4: Where has HEA been used?

Agricultural	Mozambique, Malawi, Swaziland, Zambia, Lesotho, Zimbabwe, Tanzania, Ethiopia, Rwanda, Burundi, Democratic Republic of Congo (DRC), Southern Sudan, Sudan, Niger, Mali, Liberia, Sierra Leone, Tajikistan, Bangladesh, India, Pakistan, Cambodia, Myanmar (Burma), Chechnya
Pastoralist/agro-pastoralist	Somalia, Somaliland, Southern Sudan, Sudan, Ethiopia, Angola, Djibouti, Tanzania, Kenya, Burkina Faso
Urban	Angola, Zimbabwe (Harare), Djibouti (Djibouti City), Somaliland (Hargeisa), Somalia (Belet Weyne), north Sudan (Khartoum), occupied Palestinian territory, Kosovo, Serbia, Montenegro, Macedonia, DRC (Bunia, Kinshasa)
Coastal (including fishing) communities	India, Indonesia, Sri Lanka, Somalia
Refugee camps	Kenya, Bangladesh, Sudan, Tanzania, Ethiopia, Chad, Uganda
Internally displaced persons (IDPs)	Burundi, Southern Sudan, Somalia, Khartoum, Liberia, Ingushetia

Table 5: Uses of HEA and examples of different applications

Application	Case study	Which part of the HEA framework is involved?
Disaster preparedness, relief and recovery		
Designing **early warning and monitoring** systems (section 3.1)	**Rural** Malawi: MVAC Ethiopia **Urban** Harare: Urban monitoring system	• **Baseline** helps identify what people in a livelihood zone are vulnerable to so that relevant parameters can be monitored • **Outcome analysis** undertaken at key points of year, using monitoring data to define the problem

continued opposite

Table 5 *continued*

Application	Case study	Which part of the HEA framework is involved?
Disaster preparedness, relief and recovery *continued*		
Developing scenarios for **contingency and response planning** (section 3.2)	Limpopo Basin, Mozambique, Serbia	• **Outcome analysis** used to develop scenarios and identify indicators for monitoring and updating of response plans
Assessing **emergency food and non-food needs** (section 3.3)	Mashonaland, Zimbabwe	• **Outcome analysis** used to measure current and projected access against thresholds
Post-emergency **rehabilitation** (section 3.3)	Earthquake recovery, Pakistan	• **Baseline** and **outcome analysis** used to map out pre-crisis livelihood strategies and post-crisis opportunities
Poverty reduction and social protection		
Identifying appropriate **poverty reduction** strategies (section 3.4)	Thar Desert, Pakistan Tigray, Ethiopia	• **Baseline** used to identify constraints and opportunities for different wealth groups and strategies for minimising/ exploiting them
Designing a **safety net transfer programme** (section 3.5)	Turkana, Kenya	• **Baseline** used to determine gap between current and desired standard of living and to identify complementary policies
Modelling the impact of **other social protection measures** (section 3.5)	Singida, Tanzania Djibouti Turkana, Kenya	• **Baseline** used to analyse changes to income and expenditure patterns • **Baseline** used to analyse impact of rising cost of particular items of expenditure
Identifying **constraints to health and education** (section 3.5)	Singida, Tanzania	• **Baseline** used to compare costs of health and education with available income

continued overleaf

Table 5 continued

Application	Case study	Which part of the HEA framework is involved?
Poverty reduction and social protection continued		
Identifying appropriate **market support** interventions (section 3.6)	Upper Limpopo, Mozambique Market-led Livelihoods for Vulnerable Populations (MLVP), Ethiopia	• **Baseline** used to identify areas of potential for different wealth groups and key market constraints
Monitoring and evaluation		
Monitoring and evaluating the impact of interventions on households (section 3.7)	Tigray, Ethiopia MLVP, Ethiopia	• **Baseline** used to establish targets for food and income generation and as starting point against which to measure impact • **Outcome analysis** used to show which hazards might interfere with reaching targets

3.1 Using HEA in the design of early warning and monitoring systems

Conceived as a framework for estimating the likely impact of a shock on household access to food and income, the HEA framework has been used as the basis for early warning and monitoring systems in both rural and urban areas.

Early warning in rural areas

Early warning in much of southern Africa is set in a context of fragile livelihoods, low and deteriorating resources and assets, and shocks. In terms of rain failure, the most common event is not catastrophic drought but the 'bad year' that pushes many poor households over the hunger threshold. In such environments, early warning efforts require sensitivity to differences which may appear marginal between localities and between households. There must be an ability to discern whether a small shock might result in a significant food security problem,

> In the southern African context of widespread chronic food insecurity, early warning needs to be sensitive to the very fine difference between poverty and livelihood failure.

and conversely whether the market may in some circumstances mitigate the effects of even a relatively large shock. There must be an ability to predict the effect of economic shocks, such as steep rises in the price of grain or the collapse of cash crop prices. And increasingly, systems must give early warning not just of hunger, but of acute impoverishment where people cannot cover essential non-food needs. A system with the capacity to discern the fine differences in household response and ability to cope allows more considered choices about the intervention to be made.

At the same time, programme planners require significant lead time to set up resource and logistical flows and, once these are established, they need to know how long assistance will be needed. The longer the lead time, the less expensive the delivery of goods tends to be, and the more beneficial the effects.

HEA attempts to satisfy both these requirements and offer a form of analysis that both takes into account the variations in livelihoods and response among different households, and projects ahead of time what such variations might mean in terms of programme planning. Through the use of scenario analysis, HEA is able to predict how big or small food and income deficits will be even if the effects take time to set in.

HEA has been used to design livelihoods-based national food security early warning systems in southern Sudan, Somalia and Malawi, and is being integrated into the national early warning system in Ethiopia. It has also been used for cross-country analysis in the Sahel. Its application in Malawi is described below.

• THE HOUSEHOLD ECONOMY APPROACH

> **Case study: Using HEA for early warning of food insecurity in Malawi**[5]
>
> Since 2003, Malawi's Vulnerability Assessment Committee (MVAC) has used HEA as the basis for estimating emergency food and/or cash needs. Projections are made in March/April, providing humanitarian agencies with a lead time of eight to nine months.
>
> Projections use baseline livelihoods data, which was compiled in 2003 for most of the country. This means that ongoing annual assessment activities in March and April can focus on the cross-checking and refining of crop production estimates – of both cereal and cash crops – and of other 'hazard' information such as changes in the price of maize, cotton or tobacco, or changes in the availability of *ganyu* (local casual employment). Different scenarios are generated, on the basis of assumptions about grain prices in the December to February period.
>
> The end result is a projection of food security needs across the country based explicitly on an analysis of households' access to food – that is, taking into account all their sources of food and income, their assets, and their patterns of expenditure – rather than solely their production.
>
> The initial investment in obtaining livelihoods baselines pays off year after year as it continues to be the basis for projections and planning.

Monitoring food insecurity and poverty in urban areas

The HEA framework has also been used to establish systems for the monitoring of urban livelihoods in Harare, Djibouti and Hargeisa. Urban assessments using HEA have been carried out in these cities and more widely (see Table 4: Where has HEA been used?'), for one of two purposes: either to learn more about the burgeoning urban population, and especially the conditions in the poorest areas and shanty towns; or to assess need following internal conflict or urban unrest.

There are important differences between urban and rural livelihoods, which have implications for how they should be monitored. Perhaps the most important is relative inability of urban households to produce their own food and their heavy dependence on the market. This means that poor urban populations are highly vulnerable to changes in market conditions and especially to changes in the price of basic food and non-food commodities. Another important difference is that sources of income among poor urban households are relatively heterogeneous compared with those of rural households, making it more difficult to track changes in income – as is commonly done in monitoring systems in rural areas. On the other hand, patterns of expenditure tend to be more homogeneous, so that changes in expenditure are generally easier to monitor than changes in income.

The case study below shows how HEA was used to help design a practical monitoring system in Harare in 2001.

Case study: Using HEA to monitor food security and poverty in Harare[6]

In 2001 the USAID Famine Early Warning System (FEWS NET) and the Consumer Council of Zimbabwe (CCZ) carried out an assessment of urban vulnerability in greater Harare. One aim of this assessment was to recommend a practical monitoring system that provided an early indication of declining access to food and essential cash income.

The assessment team recommended a two-pronged approach, involving the monitoring of both expenditure and income. On the one side, patterns of expenditure for poorer families were translated into 'expenditure baskets', the costs of which could be tracked over time. On the other side, a monthly survey of incomes and profits among informal businesses was proposed, as well as the monitoring of incomes in the formal sector.

continued overleaf

Case study: Using HEA to monitor food security and poverty in Harare *continued*

An example of how this information was used later in 2001 is given in Figure 8. This shows the rise in the cost of the expenditure baskets for three wealth groups.

Parallel monitoring of formal sector wages showed an increase in wages that lagged far behind such price increases. The picture for the informal sector was mixed, with income from some businesses keeping pace with inflation, while others lagged behind.

Figure 8: The rising costs of household expenditure baskets in Harare, September 2001 compared with May 2001

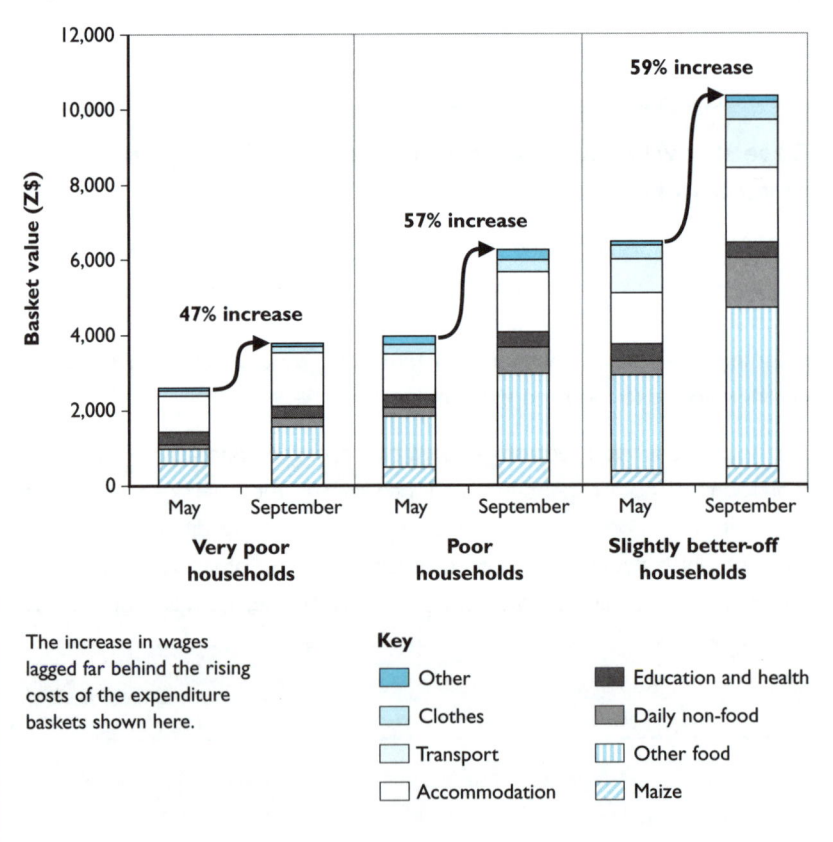

The increase in wages lagged far behind the rising costs of the expenditure baskets shown here.

Key
- Other
- Clothes
- Transport
- Accommodation
- Education and health
- Daily non-food
- Other food
- Maize

The main shock to which households in Harare were vulnerable in 2001 was inflation – in the price of rents, electricity, bus fares and food – together with formal sector job losses and crackdowns on 'illegal' businesses in the informal sector, which resulted in the loss of tools, goods and capital.

In contrast, an HEA-based livelihoods monitoring system in Djibouti City, set up in 2003 following an HEA assessment, was designed to monitor changes in a very different city: an important Red Sea port and international military base. Here, an important determinant of income in poor households is the availability of casual labour, which is largely dependent on activity in the port and within the construction sector. Government policy can have a significant impact on livelihoods, not just through its influence on incomes (through changes in salaries and pensions) and on expenditure (through pricing policy), but through its policy on migration. In 2003, the expulsion of foreign migrants reduced both the competition for low-paid work and the demand for basic goods and services. All these factors were incorporated into the HEA-based monitoring system. One of the ways in which the system helped effect a change in government policy is described in the case study on Djibouti City in section 3.5.

3.2 Using HEA in contingency and response planning

Early warning is a necessary activity in preventing food crises, but is not in itself sufficient. To achieve a prompt and appropriate response, early warning should trigger the implementation of contingency plans. HEA can also be used to examine the likely effects of hazards that may occur at an indeterminate time in the future and thus can be a useful aid in disaster preparedness.

The process of contingency planning involves, first, identifying exactly which contingencies need to be planned for, on the basis of a clear understanding of the hazards facing a population and the population's vulnerability to them. Second, scenarios need to be developed for each contingency, showing what will happen as the result of a particular event: how many people will be affected? How will they be affected? Where are they?

Scenario-building is perhaps the most difficult step in the contingency planning process, because it involves defining what will happen in the future. Scenarios have to be based on a number of assumptions, which, as events unfold, will seldom remain valid; contingency plans can quickly become outdated unless the original assumptions are monitored and plans adjusted accordingly.

HEA has been used in a range of contexts to develop scenarios for use within the contingency planning process. Typically, two or more scenarios are developed to reflect possible trends in prices or other factors. For example, the Malawi VAC's food security projections for 2004/05, described in the case study in section 3.1 above, were calculated for two different price scenarios over the purchasing period from December to March.

Importantly, HEA helps to identify what should be monitored in order to update and refine initial projections. HEA-based scenarios are not intended as the final word on projected needs; rather, they are a means of providing a first estimate that, through agreed monitoring indicators, can be refined and adjusted as events proceed.

Case study: Using HEA for contingency planning in the Limpopo River Basin[7]

After the disastrous floods of 2000 in the Limpopo Basin, Mozambique, three organisations collaborated to develop an Atlas for Disaster Preparedness and Response. This mapped communities, roads, schools, population, hazard risk and livelihoods, creating a detailed baseline for disaster preparedness and response. Scenarios for drought, cyclones and floods modelled the impact of these hazards on a range of areas such as infrastructure, food access, crop production, livelihoods and housing. HEA was used to model impacts on food security.

For example, one scenario suggested that, in the event of future flooding, food aid requirements would be very limited both in quantity and duration. Only the relatively small percentage of households living along the river basin itself were found likely to be affected by floods; 80% of households lived on sandier soils in higher areas and produced most of their own food from plots there. Most households in the area also derived significant cash income from

continued opposite

Case study: Using HEA for contingency planning in the Limpopo River Basin *continued*

remittances from the mines in South Africa and, after a flood, would be able to purchase food with this money as soon as food became available in the market. In addition, affected households would replant along the river once flood waters had receded, and so would be able to harvest their own crops three months later.

This analysis provided an estimate of the maximum food aid tonnage that would be required, on the assumption that it could be refined and reduced according to monitoring results.

HEA has also been used to develop scenarios in predominantly urban situations for which contingency planners need to model the effects not of natural hazards, but of future macro-level economic events and related price changes. In the case study below, HEA was used to develop projections of the numbers of pensioners in need of assistance according to different government policy decisions. This case study also shows that the assumptions used in any particular HEA analysis are explicit, allowing them to be challenged and adjusted according to changing circumstances.

Case study: Using HEA for contingency planning in a shifting macroeconomic context – Serbia[8]

In March 2000, the World Food Programme (WFP) of the United Nations commissioned an HEA assessment in Serbia to identify which groups were food insecure and to determine the levels of assistance needed throughout the coming year. The assessment focused on the urban areas and the population groups considered to be most in need, looking in particular at pensioners and their dependants.

continued opposite

• THE HOUSEHOLD ECONOMY APPROACH

Case study: Using HEA for contingency planning in a shifting macroeconomic context – Serbia *continued*

The analysis combined baseline data with information on possible future trends (such as in food prices) to project food aid needs over the year. Because of uncertainty over the future price of food and basic non-food items, and in particular over the future of the government's price control system, three scenarios were developed, based on combinations of how prices would move relative to pension levels. Estimates of numbers of people in need were then made, considering the implications of including or excluding the use of people's own coping strategies, giving six possible outcomes in total. The projected numbers in need under each of these scenarios are shown in Figure 10.

Figure 9: Scenario projections in Serbia, 2000

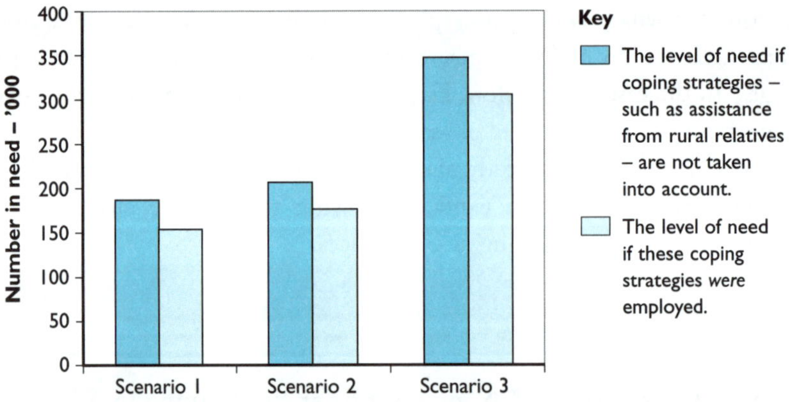

Key
- The level of need if coping strategies – such as assistance from rural relatives – are not taken into account.
- The level of need if these coping strategies *were* employed.

Scenario 1: Best case
The value of the pension keeps pace with the cost of the minimum basket of food and non-food items; ie, government controls rate of inflation.

Scenario 2: Middle case
The value of the pension keeps pace with changes in controlled prices but not free market prices; ie, a continuation of the situation over previous two years.

Scenario 3: Worst case
The controlled price system collapses with resulting sharp increases in the prices of controlled items.

3.3 Using HEA in needs assessments

Central to the challenge of responding effectively to humanitarian crises is the question: how can assessment practice be improved? How can we achieve a more consistent and accurate picture of the scale and nature of the problems that people in crisis face, and ensure that decisions about response are properly informed by that understanding? The lack of a system-wide, transparent method for prioritising response has been identified as a major problem and a contributing factor to the inequitable allocation of humanitarian resources across different contexts. There is a recognised need for greater consistency in the way problems are framed, in terms of observable symptoms, proximate causes and acute risk factors.[9]

Two other points about food security assessments in particular are relevant here. First, there is a consensus that they should provide a basis for determining a broader range of intervention options than at present, including those that seek to tackle chronic food insecurity. HEA's contribution to this area is discussed in sections 3.4 and 3.5. Second, it has been suggested that they should distinguish more clearly between situations where the primary rationale for food assistance is to save lives, and situations where the main rationale is to protect assets or livelihoods.[10]

The case studies from Mashonaland overleaf and Pakistan described later in this section illustrate how HEA can bring the following strengths to needs assessment:

- Using a relatively simple and conceptually clear framework, HEA provides a quantified comparison of current or predicted access to food and cash income with different thresholds. These thresholds relate to the requirements for either survival or livelihoods protection (see section 2.5).
- Quantification of food and income in absolute terms (kilocalories accessed and cash earned) means that comparisons between different wealth groups and different areas can be made, which facilitates prioritisation of resources.
- Because HEA is based on a holistic view of livelihoods – estimating the effect of change on both food and cash income, and on the need to sell assets or forgo non-food expenditure (which also takes into account the role of markets) – it enables a range of possible interventions to be identified.

• THE HOUSEHOLD ECONOMY APPROACH

Emergency needs assessment

The following case study illustrates how HEA can provide a quantitative, comparative picture of the immediate needs of communities with very different livelihoods, together with a qualitative analysis of the fundamental problems facing each community and the risks to which they are vulnerable. It also shows the importance of being able to model the effects of more than one hazard.

In this case, the very high rate of inflation meant that the most appropriate form of relief was food aid, rather than cash or vouchers. In other situations, HEA has – sometimes in conjunction with more in-depth market assessments – helped to identify the appropriate balance of response between food and cash relief.

This was the case with an HEA assessment carried out in Pakistan in 2005,[11] which was tasked with considering the impact of the October earthquake on livelihoods in parts of Azad Jammu and Kashmir. The analysis highlighted the importance of markets both within and outside the area to the pre-earthquake rural economy, which was highly cash-based and strongly linked to urban

---

Case study: Using HEA to assess the needs of different communities affected by macroeconomic change – Mashonaland, Zimbabwe[12]

As part of a series of food security assessments across southern Africa following the 2001/02 drought, HEA assessments were carried out in the Mashonaland Provinces of Zimbabwe in July and August 2002. The assessments focused on communities that were vulnerable to changes in the wider macroeconomic and policy climate, such as the land reform programme and rising food prices, as well as to drought. One of the objectives was to assess households' ability to access food and non-food items and services at that time, and to predict how this might change over the following eight months. The analysis showed how access to food over the four months prior to the assessment varied between the different communities (see Figure 10).

continued opposite

Case study: Using HEA to assess the needs of different communities affected by macroeconomic change – Mashonaland, Zimbabwe *continued*

Figure 10: Patterns of food access for households in Mashonaland, Zimbabwe

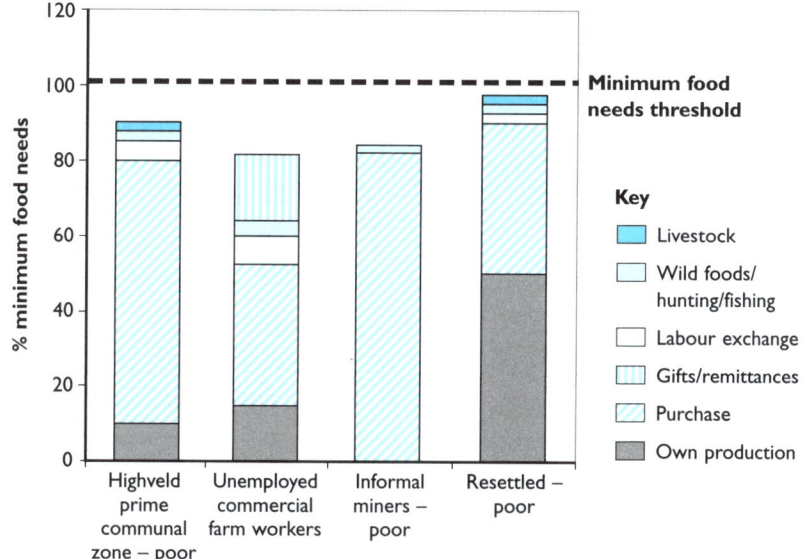

The poor in the highveld communal zone
One of the most prosperous areas of communal lands. But the poor have been affected by (i) drought, reducing own crop production and labouring opportunities; (ii) land reform, reducing labouring opportunities on neighbouring commercial farms; and (iii) high inflation rates for essential items.
• **Need for improved input provision.**

Unemployed commercial farm workers
No formal income, and no access to the casual work provided by newly-settled farmers, who tend to favour fellow resettlers. Gifts/remittances from relatives on neighbouring farms will dry up as more farms close.
• Livelihoods are entirely income-based and **very vulnerable to inflation**.

Informal miners
Used to depend on seasonal employment on the neighbouring commercial farms to compensate for seasonal drop in mining income. With the closure of so many farms, this source of cash is no longer open to mining families.
• Not vulnerable to drought but **very vulnerable to inflation**.

Resettled farmers
Tend to be more food secure than neighbouring farmers in the communal areas. But they lacked the inputs to cultivate more than 20–50% of their allocated land.
• **Urgent need for agricultural input credits and improved infrastructure.**

centres through employment and remittances. In terms of the balance between food and cash relief, the assessment recommended that:
- As markets gradually began to function again, remaining food relief needs should be addressed by a **gradual substitution of cash for in-kind food aid**.
- Until families had rebuilt shelters in villages, or been provided with semi-permanent shelter in camps, **free relief was more appropriate than 'for-work'** interventions.
- **Cash-for-work activities** could be considered after shelter had been restored, although more employment was likely to be available by that time.
- If agencies went ahead with **food-for-work activities**, they should consider both the labour supply in the household plus the need for families to have cash to purchase non-food needs.

Post-emergency needs assessment: livelihoods support and recovery

HEA has also been used in post-emergency assessments that seek to identify ways of helping livelihoods to recover. Because an analysis of livelihoods prior to a crisis is central to HEA – even if this analysis has to be done retrospectively – the method has been found helpful in highlighting what aspects of people's livelihoods need support following a crisis and how that could be achieved.

In such situations, the links between households of different wealth groups and the links between households and the wider economy can be particularly important. This is illustrated in the following case study.

Case study: Using HEA for livelihood support and recovery programming in Pakistan[13]

Following the earthquake of October 2005 in Pakistan, humanitarian agencies needed to find out what impact the earthquake had had on the livelihoods of different population groups, and what interventions would be effective in promoting livelihoods recovery. With its relief effort ongoing, Save the Children carried out a rapid (12-day) assessment in November in Muzaffarabad and Bagh districts.

continued opposite

Case study: Using HEA for livelihood support and recovery programming in Pakistan *continued*

The wealth breakdown and baseline analysis revealed the pre-earthquake livelihoods of different wealth groups shown in Figure 11. This enabled a better analysis of possible ways in which these different livelihoods could be restored. It also highlighted the chronic poverty of the poorest group.

Some of the findings of the analysis and their implications for programming are shown in Table 7 overleaf. Perhaps the most important message was that damage to businesses, shops and offices should be considered not as an 'exogenous' factor in relief and reconstruction activities but as central to the successful rehabilitation of livelihoods; and that household-level interventions (such as cash transfers) should be complemented with support to the market.

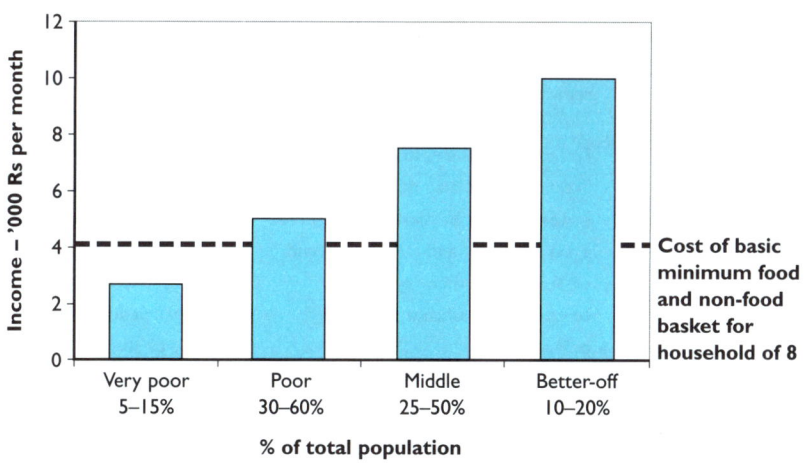

Figure 11: Income levels of four wealth groups in affected districts pre-earthquake, Pakistan

Very poor: Mainly female-headed households, relying on child labour, zakat, and some casual work.

Poor: Income largely from unskilled casual work in local towns or villages.

Middle: Income largely based on shopkeeping and small business, skilled labour, and some remittance from Pakistan's cities.

continued overleaf

Case study: Using **HEA** for livelihood support and recovery programming in Pakistan *continued*

Table 6: Implications for programming arising from the HEA analysis in Pakistan

Aspect of analysis	Finding	Implication for interventions
Disaggregated income analysis	The earthquake had affected the four groups in different ways. The **very poor and the poor** were the worst affected, as the need for men to rebuild their homes – and their reluctance to leave wives and daughters in tents – meant that they could no longer access their most significant source of income, which was employment in towns and villages. In contrast, many of the **better off** were still receiving foreign remittances or government salaries.	**Cash support** to families to rebuild their homes, both for its own sake and to allow men to go back to work. Better off are more able to meet their consumption needs.
Looking beyond the village	For the poor, the restoration of livelihoods was also dependent on **employment becoming available** again in villages and local towns, and on **food and other goods becoming available** locally as before.	**Markets should be supported** as soon as possible to get back to normal, such as through support for reconstruction and credit to shopkeepers.
Looking at seasonality of income	The poor and very poor earn little or nothing in the winter months (December to February) and **normally rely on credit** during this time. But shopkeepers were also affected and were not offering credit.	Again, **supporting local shopkeepers** to re-establish themselves will help the poor survive over the winter.

continued opposite

Case study: Using HEA for livelihood support and recovery programming in Pakistan *continued*

Table 6 *continued*

Aspect of analysis	Finding	Implication for interventions
Use of thresholds to identify the chronically poor	The poorest families were predominantly **female-headed households**. Women very rarely work outside the home in villages and, for widows, the options for making a living are extremely limited.	**Improved long-term social protection programme of regular cash transfer** and of support to keep their children in school for these and other chronically poor households.

3.4 Using HEA to inform approaches to poverty reduction

This and the following section look at how HEA has been used outside of emergency contexts, to inform different aspects of work on poverty reduction and social protection. Poverty analysis aims to inform interventions that help lift people above their current standard of living and out of poverty rather than mitigate the short-term effects of hazards. Many of the elements of poverty analysis are shared by HEA's livelihoods baseline: a consideration of the defining characteristics of the poor; of the options they have for survival and the

> HEA has been found to be helpful in informing poverty reduction work, since many of the elements of poverty analysis are shared by the HEA baseline.

• THE HOUSEHOLD ECONOMY APPROACH

seasonal patterns of their survival strategies; and of the economic and social constraints they face year on year and the origins of those constraints.

Such an understanding is essential in poverty reduction work because it is simply so difficult to identify strategies in which investment would lead to a sustainable increase in net income. The poor are constrained in every option open to them. It is very difficult for them to gain access to more land, or to produce more from the land they have, or to increase income from casual labour. Sometimes they have the means to acquire livestock, but are constrained by a shortage of land for pasture. By considering whether and how such constraints can be tackled, HEA has been used to help identify broad options for poverty reduction measures as described below.

Through a quantified picture of assets and of income and expenditure among different wealth groups, HEA also allows poverty to be measured and monitored, and thresholds to be set – as described in relation to the monitoring of poverty in Harare (see the case study in section 3.1). This in turn provides an objective framework for comparing levels of poverty across different settings and countries, as described in section 6.3.

The following case study from the Thar Desert in Pakistan illustrates how an HEA assessment can be used as a first step in identifying measures that would be effective in helping the poor. In this case, the assessment was primarily used for planning a response to a drought, but it illustrates how a baseline can suggest possible strategies for poverty reduction.

Case study: Using HEA to identify appropriate poverty reduction measures in the Thar Desert, Pakistan[14]

In the Thar Desert, wealth is determined by a combination of land and livestock ownership, which are both highly concentrated. For the poorest 60%, the only asset of any significance is their labour. Table 8 below shows the implications for longer-term poverty reduction measures arising from specific elements of the HEA analysis.

continued opposite

Case study: Using HEA to identify appropriate poverty reduction measures in the Thar Desert, Pakistan *continued*

Table 7: Implications for poverty reduction measures arising from HEA analysis in Pakistan

Assessment finding	Implication for interventions
The two central features of the household economy of the poor are the **lack of assets** – in terms of land, livestock, and education and skills – and their **dependence on credit**.	**Any poverty reduction strategy must address both the lack of assets and the problem of indebtedness** among the poor. Addressing one problem without the other will not be effective.
Land: Nearly 60% of the population own no land and cultivate the land of the better off on a sharecropping basis. This means they receive only 50–75% of the harvest.	The **ownership of land** is the single biggest reason for differences in wealth within the population. Addressing the seriously inequitable distribution of land could be very beneficial for poverty reduction. But **bringing about changes in land ownership would be extremely difficult to achieve**.
Credit: The giving and taking of loans is a central feature of this economy. In an average year, all but the better off take loans – primarily for consumption purposes rather than investment – and spend more than they earn. The **middle** group tend to have sustainable levels of debt. But the **poor** and **very poor** struggle to repay their constantly accumulating debts, which can even be passed from generation to generation.	**Programmes aimed at cancelling debts or at least swapping them for lower-interest loans** should be continued and supported. These programmes could be accompanied by savings activities, and by discussions with or sensitisation of the community regarding their spending patterns. Programmes using debt swaps to help address the issue of child labour should be extended beyond households involved with carpet-weaving.

continued overleaf

> **Case study: Using HEA to identify appropriate poverty reduction measures in the Thar Desert, Pakistan** *continued*
>
> **Table 7** *continued*
>
> | Assessment finding | Implication for interventions |
> |---|---|
> | **Livestock:** As with land, the better off sometimes have more livestock than they can look after themselves.

The practice whereby a poorer family looks after livestock in exchange for half of any offspring born, and all of the milk and butter produced, is one of the **only ways for poorer families to acquire animals** for themselves, as saving income is almost impossible. | **Accumulating livestock is one of the few ways poor households manage to acquire capital.**

This could be promoted through livestock programmes which help poor households attain small livestock that are resilient and low in maintenance costs. The establishment of small cooperatives could be considered, together with support in marketing and business skills. |
> | The **very low level of asset ownership** among the poor – especially of land and livestock but also human capital in the form of education and skills – severely limits the potential for the very poor and poor to accumulate wealth. | **Investment should be made in skills training** in sectors where there is likely to be demand – particularly in the coal-mining sector, which is expected to be developed in the district.

Investment in adequate schooling facilities should also be made to tackle the lack of literacy and basic education, which is a huge economic hindrance. |

Importantly, in considering the connections by which the poor survive, HEA offers an analysis of constraints not just in terms of a lack of assets, but in terms of the patterns of dependence and obligation by which the poor survive. Since labour is commonly the poor people's only productive asset, local relationships

> Since labour is commonly the poor's only productive asset, poverty reduction measures must be grounded in an understanding of how household labour is allocated at different periods and for what gain.

between the poor and the better off can be significant; in the Thar Desert, these relationships centre around land and credit, while in southern Africa they tend to be in relation to employment. Understanding how household labour is allocated at different periods and for what gain can be essential in ensuring that, at the very least, a poverty reduction intervention 'does no harm' in terms of adding to the work burden of men, women or children in the household. This is illustrated in the analysis of labour-poor female-headed households in Ethiopia, below.

> **Case study: Programmatic implications of an HEA analysis of poor, female-headed households in Tigray, Ethiopia**[15]
>
> Female-headed households in the Ruba Lomine project area of Tigray represent the poorest category of economically active households. Their survival patterns are particularly difficult to understand because they are constructed out of many fragmented and often hidden food and income sources. An HEA study of 1999 included a special inquiry into these households and pieced together a specific **calendar of access** that reflected the constraints faced by these women and that highlighted their remarkable capacity to exploit the smallest margins of opportunity. A comparison of monthly income and expenditure constituted part of the calendar of access and is shown in Figure 12 (overleaf). It reveals the painfully small increments by which these households survive.
>
> Two principles arose from this analysis that had clear implications for development planning: first, that these households **maximise their available labour to an extreme**; and second, that they have no **extra capital or assets to buffer them** in emergencies. Since interventions based on new income-generating activities always involve a new labour requirement, the point was made that any engagement of these households in such activities must either realise immediate returns, or be compensated in the short term by temporary assistance in the form of food or cash. In addition, these women have limited capacity to recover if they take a risk that does not prove successful. Any risks involved in taking on a new venture should be offset by the implementing agency for as long as necessary.
>
> continued overleaf

• THE HOUSEHOLD ECONOMY APPROACH

Case study: Programmatic implications of an HEA analysis of poor, female-headed households in Tigray, Ethiopia
continued

Figure 12: Comparison of income and expenditure among female-headed, labour-poor households in Tigray, Ethiopia

Income by month

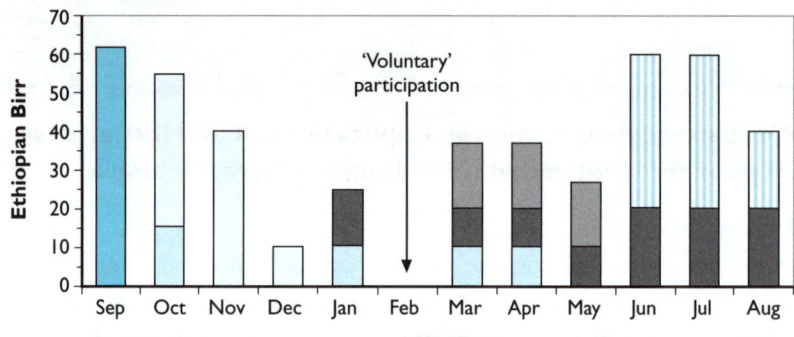

Once expenditure is taken into account, margins of 'surplus' are minimal and leave no room for missing a day of work or for unexpected expenditures on health emergencies.

Key
 Borrow    Town labour
 Handicraft    Chicks/eggs
☐ Harvest labour   ⫴ Weed labour

Expenditure by month

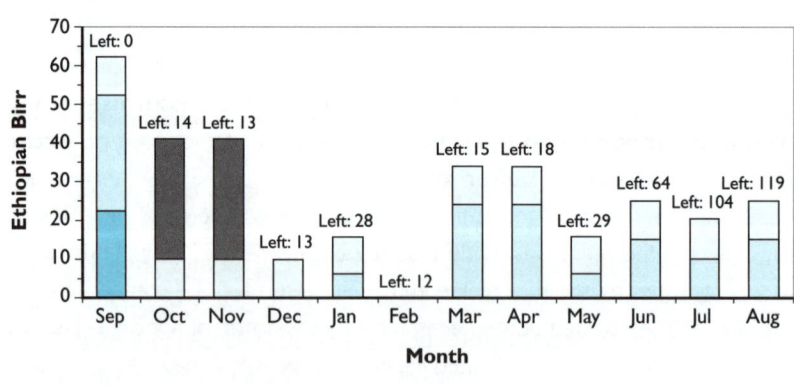

Annual expenditure on other items such as clothes, health, and fees/taxes is 117 birr, leaving 2 birr over at the end of the year.

Key
 School fees   ☐ Household items
☐ Food    Loan repayment

Such analyses are a powerful aid to poverty reduction planning. But the next sections describe how HEA has been used to go further than this and to provide more detailed guidance in the area of social protection.

3.5 Using HEA in the planning of social protection programmes

Social protection initiatives can be broadly described as those that "provide income or consumption transfers to the poor, protect the vulnerable against livelihood risks and enhance the social status and rights of the marginalised".[16] As such, the concept covers a wide range of both economic and rights-based interventions, from emergency relief and supplementary feeding, pensions, disability allowances, health insurance and agricultural input subsidies to campaigns for workers' rights. Targeted transfers to poor households, on which HEA analysis is perhaps most clearly suited to provide guidance, is just one of many possible social protection measures.

Identifying the most appropriate type of intervention in a given situation is recognised as a key challenge for vulnerability assessment methodologies. HEA does not claim to provide answers to all the questions necessary for choosing the 'right' intervention across this broad spectrum of response. But it does

> **Even interventions that seek to effect change within political, social or legal structures must be guided, and judged, by analysis at the household level.**

offer two important perspectives that can support the decision-making process. First, decisions on the most appropriate instrument – including those that seek to effect change within political, social or legal structures – must be grounded in an appreciation of the constraints and opportunities of *households* as they relate to the wider economic and political environment. The effectiveness of an intervention must also be judged by results at the *household* level. HEA offers such a form of analysis. Second, HEA can model the potential impact of different interventions on the household economy, especially in terms of asset ownership and households' ability to afford particular expenditures. This enables decision-makers to compare the possible effects of different measures.

The rest of this section first describes how HEA has been used in the **design of a safety net transfer**, specifically in determining the level and duration of transfer required to achieve a particular objective, and the target population. This is followed by an outline of how HEA has been used to **identify and model the impact of other social protection interventions**, including those that aim to address structural vulnerabilities such as inequitable land distribution or weak market systems. These include the enforcement of a by-law in Singida, Tanzania; a package of market-related interventions in Turkana, Kenya; and the elimination of the government's tax on kerosene in Djibouti City. Finally, this section looks at how HEA can contribute to an understanding of the **relationship between livelihoods and other sectors**, which is necessary for the planning of health and education social protection measures. Data on income and (particularly) expenditure patterns can provide insight into the economic constraints to accessing health and education. In-depth HEA analysis has also looked into the impact of chronic illness on livelihoods.[17]

Designing a safety net transfer

A safety net cash transfer represents a regular and predictable way of filling the gap between household income and a particular set of expenses or level of investment, such as that required for a defined increase in livestock ownership over a certain number of years. HEA allows the explicit modelling of different levels of transfer according to different objectives and is able to indicate at whom the transfer should be targeted and for how long, so that those objectives can be achieved. Importantly, it also helps identify other areas of intervention that are necessary alongside a transfer, to ensure a sustainable impact on poverty.

Case study: Using HEA to help analyse implementation options for a safety net[18]

In 2006, an HEA study was commissioned by Oxfam GB to analyse how a safety net transfer could be implemented in north-east Turkana, Kenya – a traditionally pastoralist area that over many years had been affected by a combination of serious rainfall shortages, insecurity and marginalisation. Herds had become too small to provide more than a minor proportion of income

continued opposite

Case study: Using HEA to help analyse implementation options for a safety net *continued*

and most households were no longer pastoralist in any economic sense. Ways in which people once coped in a crisis, such as foraging for wild foods and accepting food aid, had become normal practice. Several actors considered a safety net approach to be a more appropriate and effective way of supporting livelihoods than the annual package of food aid, cash-for-work and other aid, which had come to represent a significant proportion of income for most people.

In looking at the options for implementing a transfer, the inquiry considered the following questions:
- Could households cope on their own if aid were withdrawn?
- What level of safety net would be appropriate for this population?
- To whom should the transfer be targeted?
- For how long should the safety net run?
- What other measures are necessary?

How would households cope without aid?

The analysis found that, if all aid were cut, poor households would need to make up a deficit of nearly half their annual food energy needs. Their alternatives for doing so were found to be very limited. Some of the shortfall might be found through migration to towns (shown in Figure 13) and through

Figure 13: The food deficit arising among poor households if aid to Turkana were suspended

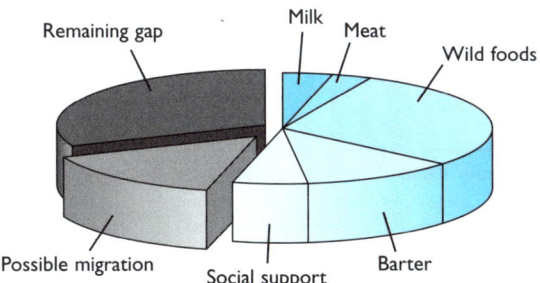

The chart shows sources of food in 2005 excluding aid, and the extent to which households might be able to make up the shortfall on their own.

continued overleaf

• THE HOUSEHOLD ECONOMY APPROACH

Case study: Using HEA to help analyse implementation options for a safety net *continued*

a very slight increase in social support and wild food collection. But to make up the full deficit – and to be able to afford their minimum non-food needs as well – they would have to sell off their entire livestock holding. In other words, surviving without aid for one year would mean destitution the next.

Calculating possible transfer levels

The analysis then considered possible levels at which a transfer could be set. A range of levels was estimated by looking at the difference between household income excluding aid and the cost of a minimum basket of food and non-food needs for a year. Figure 14 shows two possible safety net levels for poor households.

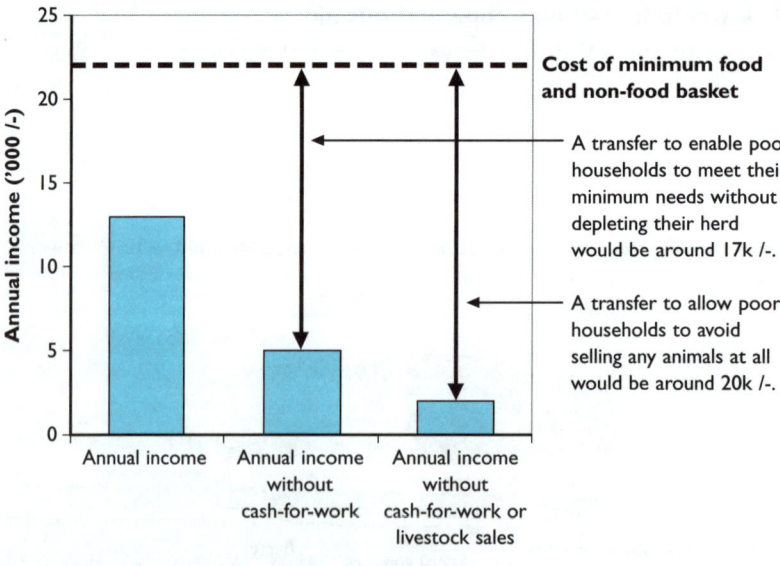

Figure 14: Two possible safety net levels for poor households in Turkana

Note: Annual income included both cash income and the change in herd value (either negative or positive) which among pastoralists also counts as income loss or gain.

continued opposite

Case study: Using HEA to help analyse implementation options for a safety net *continued*

Targeting: who should receive the transfer?

The HEA analysis had already indicated that the poor group, constituting 40–50% of the population, would not be able to cope on their own without external aid. Leaving on one side the practical and political considerations involved, the analysis then considered whether the safety net should also cover the 30–40% of the population in the middle wealth group: could they cope without aid? It was found that some could, but many could not. A safety net designed to replace food aid could, therefore, legitimately include this group, with the justification that such a transfer would make them more productive and economically independent, but in a shorter time than it would for the poor group.

For how long should the safety net run?

The HEA analysis also indicated how long the programme would have to run before herd size reached the minimum for viability. Clearly this would be different for different wealth groups. Assuming growth rates at 2005 levels, middle households would be able to build up viable herds in three years. But for the poor and very poor, this would take ten years. Phased withdrawal could, therefore, be possible for the middle group after three years, and for the poor after ten years – assuming no major changes in the economy. In other words, a commitment was needed for at least ten years, with monitoring of the wider economy essential for ensuring that progress at the household level was kept on track.

What other interventions are appropriate?

The overall aim of the study was to consider whether and how pastoralism in north-east Turkana could be 'brought back to life': that is, how households could build up their herds to a viable and sustainable level that would enable them to survive through the normal drought cycles. The study identified the underlying problems of a very low asset base, insecurity and marginalisation, and recommended other areas of intervention that would help to address these problems. These included:

continued overleaf

> **Case study: Using HEA to help analyse implementation options for a safety net** *continued*
>
> - support to improve livestock production, such as through herd improvement
> - improvement in marketing systems, including support to infrastructure (see case study on Turkana below)
> - combating political marginalisation – which would include ensuring adequate delivery of basic services
> - supporting people to leave pastoralism, especially through investment in education.
>
> Because the analysis considered households at different levels of wealth, it was able to consider a package of measures in which different kinds of support are targeted at different groups – an approach that tends to be more acceptable to the community as a whole. For example, a welfare payment to the poorest 40% of the population would be more easily accepted by the better off if it were implemented alongside a programme of animal health services targeted at the most productive households.

Modelling the impact of other social protection measures

While direct cash transfers can enable a household either to meet current consumption needs or to invest in productive capacity, other types of intervention are usually necessary to achieve a sustainable impact. HEA baseline analyses can first help to identify, and then model the impact of, measures that seek to tackle some of the structural determinants of poverty, such as lack of access to land, poor marketing systems and political marginalisation. The following case study from Tanzania illustrates how HEA has been used to model the possible effect on livelihoods of the enforcement of an existing by-law regarding access to land. The second case study from Djibouti illustrates how baseline HEA analysis helped bring about a change in taxation policy with direct and positive consequences for livelihoods. The third case study shows the possible economic return at household level of improved terms of trade, brought about by an improvement in marketing infrastructure.

3 HOW HAS HEA BEEN USED?

Case study: Using HEA in the planning of social protection interventions: Tanzania[19]

Within Tanzania, there is a national commitment to social protection as an important element of poverty reduction. In 2005, a poverty and vulnerability assessment using HEA was carried out in Singida, one of the poorest regions of Tanzania. Among other things, the information was used to model the possible effects of enforcing a district by-law that states that the minimum landholding size is four acres – about an acre more than the poor actually have access to.

Figure 15 (overleaf) shows how the poor's income and expenditure patterns might be affected if their access to land were increased by an additional acre to four acres. In the first scenario, the extra acre is used to grow a food crop. In the second, it is used to grow a cash crop.

If the extra acre were used to grow more grain, the assumption is that the household would consume more of its own harvest and would no longer have to buy grain. It would also sell any excess. This results in a net gain of 56,000 Tanzanian shillings (Tsh). Growing sunflower would have no impact on expenditure, but would lead to a 51,000 Tsh increase in income: a lower cash benefit but one that, in generating more income, gives greater spending flexibility and possibly more of a boost to the local economy.

continued overleaf

Case study: Using HEA in the planning of social protection interventions: Tanzania *continued*

Figure 15: Possible effect of additional acre of land on income and expenditure of poor households

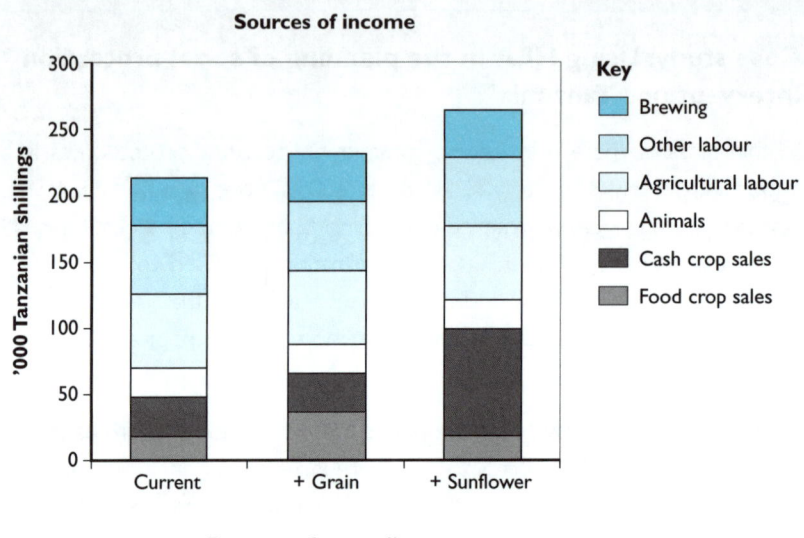

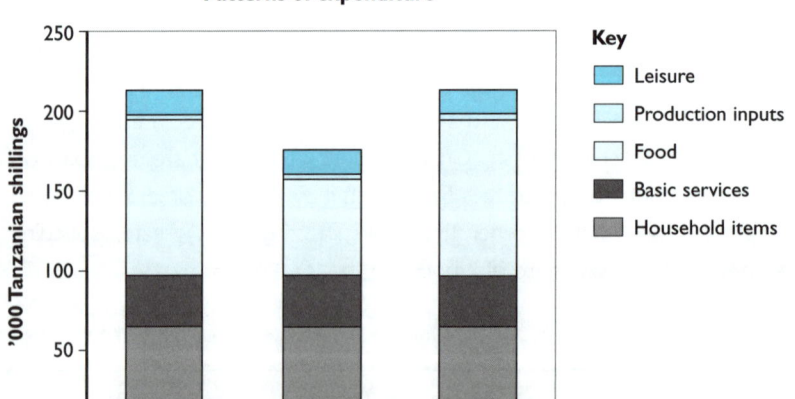

If grain is grown (+ Grain), expenditure on food can be reduced and income from food crop sales increases slightly.
If sunflowers are grown (+ Sunflower), income from cash crop sales increases and expenditure stays the same.

3 HOW HAS HEA BEEN USED?

Even the most micro-level aspects of the household economy are related in one way or another to the macro-environment. The small profit that a female-headed household makes from selling small amounts of grain across a border, for instance, is made possible because of the price differential, which rises or falls in tandem with a government-imposed import ban or production subsidy. Useful policy-related links can be drawn out of all HEA baselines, and the baseline profiling of Djibouti City provides one example of this.

Case study: How a micro-analysis helped change a macro-policy – Djibouti City[20]

In 2001, FEWS NET carried out an urban baseline assessment in Djibouti. One of the outputs of this work is presented in Figure 16, which shows the relative allocation of very poor households' income on goods and services. It shows that – surprisingly, perhaps – these households were forced to spend as much on kerosene as they did on education. Or, put another way, their spending on kerosene was limiting the amount they could invest in their children's

Figure 16: Expenditure patterns (in Djibouti francs) of very poor urban households – Djibouti 2001

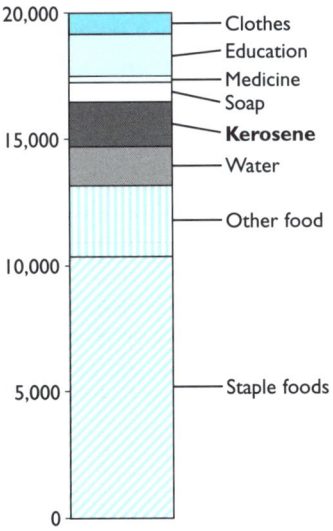

continued overleaf

• THE HOUSEHOLD ECONOMY APPROACH

> **Case study: How a micro-analysis helped change a macro-policy – Djibouti City** *continued*
>
> education, or the amount they could devote to health costs if someone in the household fell sick.
>
> The finding was important enough to compel the government to eliminate the tax on kerosene, effectively reducing its cost significantly, and freeing up a bit of extra income for these cash-strapped households.

Finally, the following example from the HEA study in Turkana illustrates how HEA can help model the potential impact at household level of a market intervention.

> **Case study: Modelling programme impact at household level, Turkana**[21]
>
> The poorly functioning markets in the Turkana area are recognised as a key constraint to economic growth. A simple HEA analysis **estimated the potential impact** of improved terms of trade on households' ability to build up their herds (see Figure 17). The quantitative estimate of outcome also provided a **basis for monitoring and evaluating the impact** on households of a package of market interventions. These included facilitating better coordination among traders, the improvement of roads and mobile phone networks, and giving traders more options on where to buy and sell.
>
> **Figure 17: Potential impact of a marketing intervention on household food access**
>
>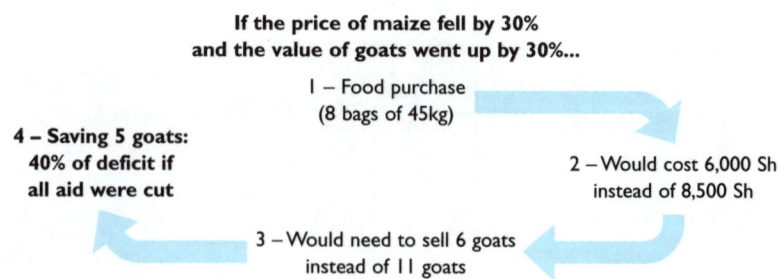
>
> If the price of maize fell by 30% and the value of goats went up by 30%...
>
> 1 – Food purchase (8 bags of 45kg)
>
> 2 – Would cost 6,000 Sh instead of 8,500 Sh
>
> 3 – Would need to sell 6 goats instead of 11 goats
>
> 4 – Saving 5 goats: 40% of deficit if all aid were cut

Understanding the relationship between livelihoods and other sectors

Poor access to services such as healthcare and education tend to be characteristics of the poor, and improved access to both is commonly a component of poverty reduction strategies. HEA has been used to look at the economic constraints that the poor face with regard to access to these sectors. Does poverty restrict access? If so, how could these constraints be tackled? The income and expenditure patterns of different wealth groups described in an HEA analysis allow the analyst to consider this question as described in the case study from Singida, Tanzania below.

Case study: Analysing the economic constraints in access to healthcare and education – Singida, Tanzania[22]

In Singida, Tanzania, HEA was used to analyse households' ability to pay for health services and education, and as a starting point for looking at non-economic barriers (such as quality of service) to accessing these services.

Health
The analysis found that the very poor faced considerable difficulties in paying health costs. Food alone used up around half their annual income. In particular, the analysis found that:
- The very small increments by which the poor survive from month to month militate against being able to afford a large, one-off payment
- Payment is especially difficult during the lean period, when the incidence of malaria is highest, and during which the poor rely on income from labour to meet their food needs and have no margin for other expenditure.

The analysis also considered two scenarios typically faced by households in the area – drought and the loss of the household head – and modelled the impact of these shocks on poor households' ability to pay for healthcare. This was found to be completely squeezed.

continued overleaf

Case study: Analysing the economic constraints in access to healthcare and education – Singida, Tanzania *continued*

Education

HEA was also used to look at households' ability to pay education costs. The analysis found that, although primary school fees have been abolished, the cost of uniforms and school materials remains substantial, amounting to about 10% of the income of the very poor.

But most striking is the typical cost of sending a child to secondary school. This is shown as a proportion of the annual income of different wealth groups in Figure 18; it is virtually equivalent to the annual income of the very poor and is more than one-third of the annual income of the 'middle' group. The upshot is that most households cannot afford to send a child to secondary school unless they benefit from bursaries or some other form of cost-reduction system.

Figure 18: Cost of secondary education for one child as a proportion of annual income in Singida

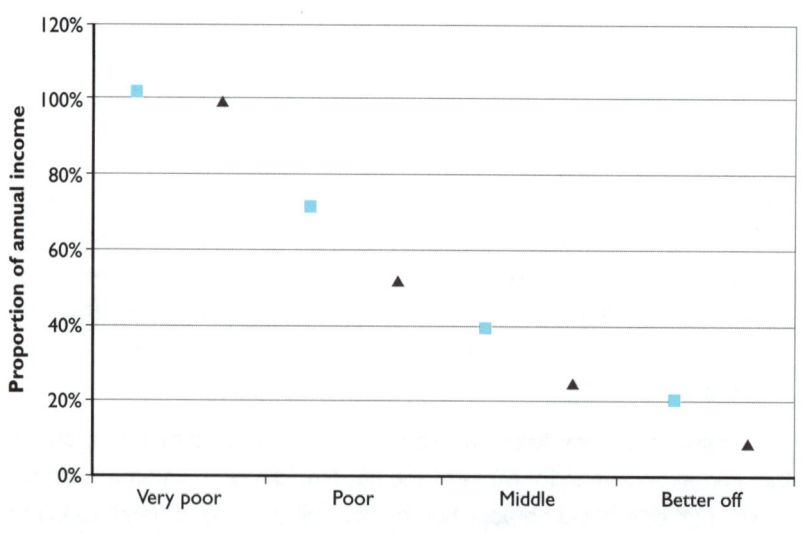

Key
- ■ Central Sandy Plains
- ▲ Iramba Plateau

It is worth noting here that a holistic approach like HEA necessarily considers the costs of healthcare or education and people's ability to afford them, whether or not the inquiry has a health or education focus. This means that HEA analyses can result in policy recommendations for these non-food sectors. This tends to occur either where the immediate balance of costs suggests a certain form of intervention (as in the case of Macedonia below), or where the future prosperity of a particular wealth group depends to a great extent on investment in education (as in the case study from Turkana, above).

> **Case study: Identifying non-food interventions – Macedonia**[23]
>
> In 2000, an assessment was carried out in Macedonia on behalf of the World Food Programme to assess the food needs of 'social cases' and to recommend phase-down/phase-up strategies for food aid distribution. Groups that were investigated included those physically unable to work, low-income pensioners, the low-income unemployed and single mothers.
>
> The assessment found that by and large these groups did not have a problem obtaining daily food. Rather, it was the large expenses such as healthcare or education costs that were difficult to meet. The conclusion was that providing support directly to the health and education sectors made more sense than the provision of free food.

3.6 Using HEA to help identify market support interventions

By building an understanding of the economic operations of households at different wealth levels and of the economic relations between them, HEA can also provide a basis for identifying market-based opportunities for economic growth and for increasing household income and assets. While many of the poorest rural areas in southern Africa face problems of land shortage, land degradation and chronically low rainfall, the urban population and urban demand expands – and interest in the use of the market to bolster rural livelihoods increases. The idea is that improving the profits gained from products and employment will at least contribute to a buffer against bad years and beyond that will be a basis for further investment in household productivity. But interventions aiming to build up households' asset base through increased engagement in the market must be grounded in a thorough understanding of current income-generating strategies, of expenditure patterns and patterns of investment, and of the opportunities and risks faced by different groups within the population.

HEA has been used in conjunction with market assessments to identify areas of investment that will help farmers generate more income through the market. What areas of the economy are farmers currently investing in, and what returns do they get? If demand exists for a particular product, how can the local market be linked to it? In Ethiopia, a USAID-funded project aiming to increase economic growth in targeted rural areas used HEA analysis in conjunction with a market study to identify four aspects of the economy which could potentially grow, given market support.[24] These included the production and sale of honey and beeswax and, for livestock owners, the sale of dairy (particularly goat) products. The market study provided the complementary analysis of potential market demand for these products.

> In conjunction with market assessments, HEA can identify market-related opportunities for growth within the household economy.

This kind of analysis identifies areas of the economy that could be expanded and, in conjunction with market assessments, the forms of market support that would be necessary, such as improving access to market information or supporting links with markets outside the area. It highlights the current limitations (why aren't farmers selling more of this product?), the possibilities (could income from this be increased if certain conditions were satisfied?), and questions and concerns that need to be addressed (can links to non-local markets be established?). Any investment in the market infrastructure that aims to effect change at the household level must be grounded in an understanding of household economic operations among different groups of the population.

The case study from Mozambique below illustrates this kind of analysis.

Case study: Using HEA to identify economic growth opportunities in markets – the Limpopo Basin, Mozambique[25]

Before the establishment of HEA baselines in the Limpopo Basin of Mozambique, the conventional wisdom was that the Upper Limpopo was semi-arid and agriculturally unproductive. Decision-makers assumed that food aid was the only option in the event of a drought or flood. What the livelihoods analysis showed was something quite different: that while this is the case in one part of the Upper Limpopo, the area where the vast majority of the population lives is highly fertile and characterised by annual crop surpluses.

The HEA analysis highlighted the real potential for households in this area, and identified the main constraint as well: lack of markets for households to sell their surpluses. All households produce more than their minimum food

Figure 19: Potential household returns on an investment in market infrastructure

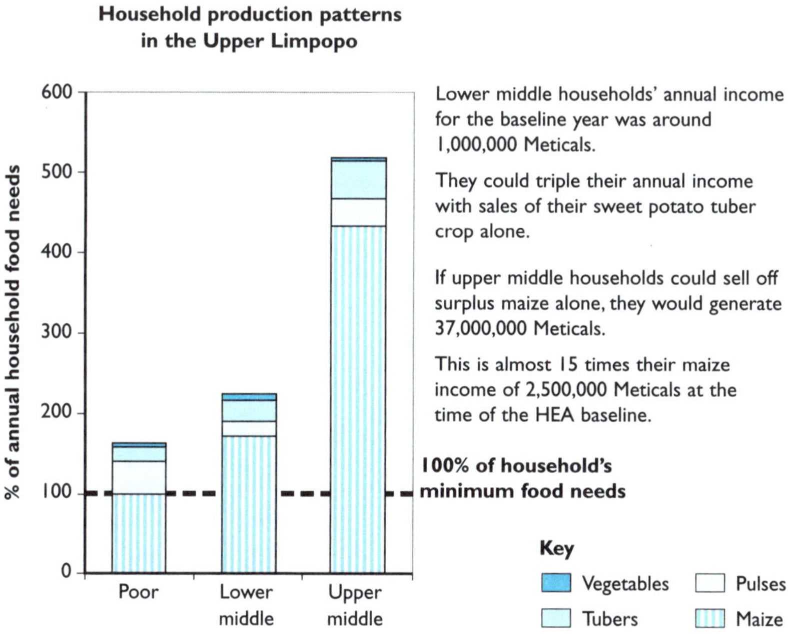
Household production patterns in the Upper Limpopo
% of annual household food needs
600
500
400
300
200
100
0
Poor
Lower middle
Upper middle
Lower middle households' annual income for the baseline year was around 1,000,000 Meticals.
They could triple their annual income with sales of their sweet potato tuber crop alone.
If upper middle households could sell off surplus maize alone, they would generate 37,000,000 Meticals.
This is almost 15 times their maize income of 2,500,000 Meticals at the time of the HEA baseline.
100% of household's minimum food needs
Key
Vegetables
Pulses
Tubers
Maize

continued overleaf

• THE HOUSEHOLD ECONOMY APPROACH

> **Case study: Using HEA to identify economic growth opportunities in markets – the Limpopo Basin, Mozambique** continued
>
> requirements in a typical year. Better-off households, which claim that much of their surplus goes to waste because of both poor storage capacity and their inability to sell as much as they would like, could substantially expand their economic opportunities if they could market their surpluses, as shown in Figure 19. Poor roads and limited marketing infrastructure mean that a substantial economic growth potential goes untapped in this area. It is clear that economic development in the Upper Limpopo area rests in large part on a better link to the Maputo market.

3.7 Using HEA in project design, monitoring and evaluation

The holistic view of household economy that HEA offers also lends itself to being used for monitoring programme impact. The challenge of impact assessment and monitoring – that is, measuring outcomes rather than tracking the distribution of inputs – applies especially to programmes that have an explicit objective to support and promote livelihoods. It is hard enough to monitor, say, the additional cash earned by households that can be directly attributed to a livelihoods programme; or to monitor what households do with that cash. It is harder still to measure and monitor the implications of such changes for livelihoods as a whole.

HEA's strengths in impact monitoring are, first, that it offers a **holistic** view of livelihoods. The analysis allows a focus on a particular aspect of the household economy – say, food production – and how that might change, but always in the context of other sources of food and income and of expenditure needs. Second, components of the household economy are **quantified** and, therefore, amenable to monitoring over time.

> HEA can be useful in impact monitoring because it offers a holistic and quantified view of livelihoods.

Given these two characteristics, HEA is able to offer three different perspectives of programme impact:
- the impact on the household economy and access to services and, by extension, on household poverty (How have targeted households benefited from the project or policy? Have there been negative effects?)
- the impact on poverty at the community level (has there been a shift in membership of wealth groups?)
- the impact of the programme relative to other changes that have been happening, so that non-programme influences are explicitly recognised and taken into account. Importantly, this enables programme managers to judge in advance the likely effects of unforeseen shocks, such as drought, and to take action to mitigate them in appropriate ways.

The following case studies illustrate how this has been done in practice.

Assessing project impact at the household level

Where an intervention comprises a number of different strands (such as a development programme) or is expected to have multiple impacts (a cash transfer, for example, is likely to affect the household economy in a number of ways), a holistic approach to impact assessment is essential. One attempt to assess impact using HEA is illustrated in the following case study. In this inquiry, HEA was also used to offer strategic direction to the programme, indicating the potential profit for poorer people from project outcomes other than food production, particularly through livestock and timber activities.

Case study: Assessing the impact on livelihoods of a rural development programme, Tigray, Ethiopia

In 2001, an HEA assessment was carried out on behalf of Oxfam-Canada and the Relief Society of Tigray (REST) in the Ruba Lomine project area of Tigray, Ethiopia. One of the aims of the assessment was to develop tools for monitoring the change in household income and food access as a result of the programme. Project impact had usually been reported in terms of the

continued overleaf

Case study: Assessing the impact on livelihoods of a rural development programme, Tigray, Ethiopia *continued*

distribution of inputs such as vegetable seeds and tools. The missing element was the impact of these inputs on household food security.

The HEA study focused on how the impact of three project outputs could be monitored: vegetable gardens, tree sales and fodder development. A 'toolbox' of monitoring tools was compiled for each. Some of the questions that could be asked as a means of monitoring the impact on livelihoods of vegetable gardens, for example, are shown in the box.

- Assessing the impact on livelihoods of vegetable gardens
- How much was produced in a good and a bad year?
- How much was eaten and how much sold?
- What were the labour requirements?
- What other activities suffer because of the garden work?
- How much was earned on average per week?
- How much is this as a proportion of the family's normal annual income?
- Are there limits to the demand in the markets where the vegetables are sold?

A key factor enabling this monitoring was a baseline household economy survey conducted in 1999. This provided the baseline data against which changes in income, expenditure and labour requirements could be measured. The analysis enabled change to be interpreted in the context of the household economy as a whole, on the basis of a typical annual income or typical seasonal expenditure. For example, an increase in income of 40 birr represented a 2% increase for labour-rich households, but a 10% increase for a labour-poor, female-headed household. It was less significant if converted into food equivalents, as it represented only about two to three weeks' food for the whole family. The impact on food security was small. The analysis showed that, nevertheless, 40 birr per year would have important social impacts if used to send an additional child to school.

Assessing shifts in asset ownership within a community

HEA can also be used to assess whether there has been a shift in asset ownership or in the membership of wealth groups. It can also help to identify the *causes* of observed shifts. This is important as it helps to distinguish between changes in wealth patterns that are slow and structural, and those that are rapid and linked to a recent disaster.

Figure 20 compares HEA data from 2000 with data from 1970 in one part of Tigray, Ethiopia, and shows a trend towards impoverishment over those 30 years. But the livelihoods data showed that this did not mean that the villages had become more vulnerable to crop failure. Rather, in 2000 the poor were sustained in their villages not by local transfers as in the past – when wealth was produced locally – but by capital from outside the area. This capital came mainly from migrant labourers working in neighbouring regions, and also from food aid paid out to labourers on public work schemes or food-for-work schemes.

Figure 20: Changes in wealth breakdown in Dabano, Tigray between 1970/71 and 2000/01

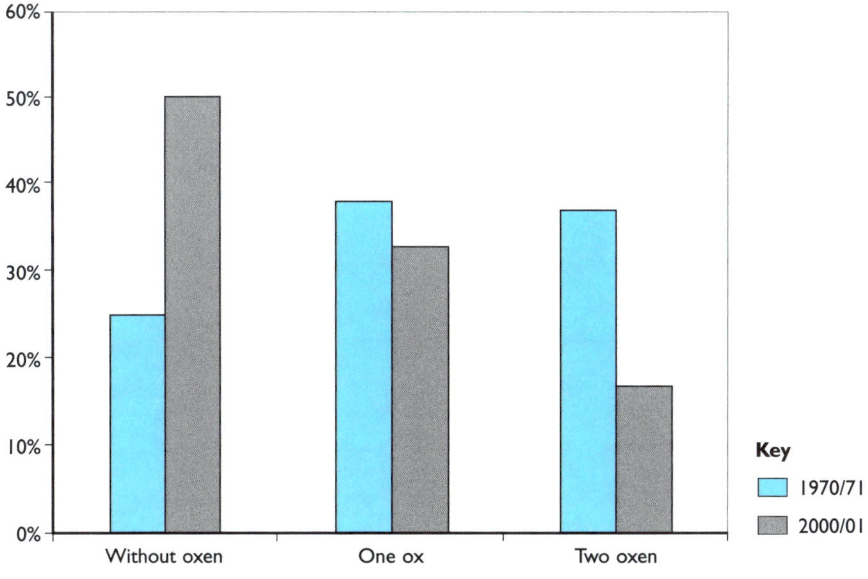

Source: Holt and Bush (2001)

• THE HOUSEHOLD ECONOMY APPROACH

Assessing project impact relative to other changes

HEA also enables analysis of the possible impact of multiple changes. For instance, what happens to household incomes in a year when harvests are down by 50% but fodder supplies, from enclosed project areas, are up by 200%? The example below shows how the disaggregated analysis which HEA offers can help not just in monitoring impact, but in project implementation, by indicating to programme managers in advance the likely effect of a shock such as drought or price rises on project impact. This allows programme managers to plan mitigation activities that will help keep the project on track, rather than having to deal with the effects of the shock retrospectively.

In the design of the USAID-funded Market-led Livelihoods for Vulnerable Populations (MLVP) project, HEA was identified as a means of monitoring project impact and predicting the likely effects on this of a shock such as drought, thereby enabling programme managers to plan for this in advance, as shown in Figure 21.

Figure 21: Using HEA to help identify project thresholds

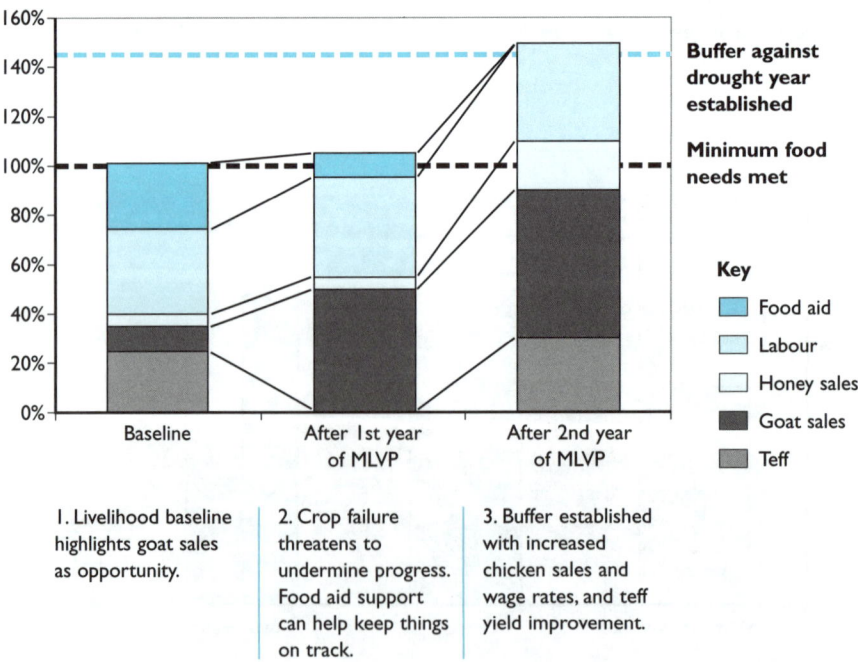

1. Livelihood baseline highlights goat sales as opportunity.
2. Crop failure threatens to undermine progress. Food aid support can help keep things on track.
3. Buffer established with increased chicken sales and wage rates, and teff yield improvement.

Source: Chemonics Int. with FEG (2004)

4 How is HEA done?

Since its inception, HEA has been strongly associated with rapid appraisal methods, particularly the use of semi-structured interviews with key informants and focus groups. In all the contexts in which HEA has been applied over the past decade, this has been the way in which the information has been collected, for reasons discussed in Chapter 5. The present chapter outlines how and at what level (national, district or village) these methods are used for different steps in the framework. While assessments vary to some extent according to the staff and time available, and according to factors such as security and access, there are certain principles and practices which have emerged from the field experience of the past 15 years that can help guide an HEA enquiry and ensure a minimum level of quality control. These practices and procedures are described in more detail in *The Practitioners' Guide to HEA*, Chapter 3, 'Baseline assessment'.

It should be noted, however, that HEA is an analytical framework that can use data gathered by any method or combination of methods to allow the construction of a logical and consistent picture of livelihoods among different groups and in different areas, within the required timescale and with the resources available. It can, thus, use data from household sample surveys just as it can use data gathered through rapid appraisal, provided, in both cases, quality control measures can be put in place. The HEA framework is clear and specific about the questions that need to be asked; the way in which the answers are obtained is, in contrast, a matter of resources, practicalities and the relative merits of different methods in each context.

> HEA is an analytical framework that requires both qualitative and quantitative data in order to produce a practical output useful for decision-making.
>
> This data is usually collected through what in social science parlance are called qualitative research techniques.

The strong association of HEA with rapid appraisal has sometimes led to confusion over whether HEA is a qualitative or a quantitative method. In social science there is a distinction made between quantitative and qualitative methods: "Qualitative research is a set of research techniques in marketing and social sciences in which data are obtained from a relatively small group of respondents and not analyzed with statistical techniques. This differentiates it from quantitative research in which a large group of respondents provide data that are statistically analyzed."[26] Thus, HEA information – which includes both qualitative and quantitative data – tends to be collected using qualitative rather than quantitative research techniques.

4.1 How is HEA information collected?

As described in Chapter 2, there are six steps in the HEA framework. The table opposite indicates how information is gathered or put together for each of these steps.

An HEA investigation tends to work step by step from the wider level down to the village and household level. It starts from the 'big picture' at national or provincial level (what is the general pattern of livelihoods in different areas?) and then at district level (how do people get by in general terms in this area?). It then works through an analysis of access to resources and definitions of poverty at village or community level (how does access to land and livestock affect livelihood strategies? What does it mean to be poor in this area?), to a detailed inquiry among household representatives into exactly how people at different levels of wealth get by.

How is a livelihood zoning done?

It is generally not possible to delineate livelihood zones on the basis of secondary data alone, because livelihood zones are not based on what the land is used for (as shown on a land use map) or on what people grow (as shown on an agro-ecological map), but on what people do.

The steps in a livelihood zoning are usually:
1. A review of available rainfall, agro-ecological, soil, vegetation and agro-economic maps.
2. An initial workshop at either national or regional level to obtain a preliminary map and zone descriptions. Participants usually include technical staff from relevant line ministries (eg, agriculture, livestock, meteorology, natural resources, fishing), NGOs and international organisations.

4 HOW IS HEA DONE?

Table 8: How information is gathered for each step in HEA

	Steps in HEA	What is it?	Where does the information come from?
BASELINE	Livelihood zoning	Defining areas within which people share broadly the same patterns of livelihood	Review of secondary data, national or provincial workshops and meetings, and district-level key informant interviews
	Wealth breakdown	Grouping people together using local definitions of wealth and quantifying their assets	Semi-structured interviews with district key informants and community leaders
	Analysis of livelihood strategies	Quantifying people's sources of food and income and their expenditure patterns	Semi-structured interviews with representatives from households within each wealth group
OUTCOME ANALYSIS	Analysis of hazard	Translating a hazard or other shocks into economic consequences at household level	Information on hazards is gained from (1) routinely collected monitoring data collected through, for example, agriculture- and price-monitoring systems; (2) seasonal assessments and targeted field inquiry; and (3) other sources such as remote sensing.
	Analysis of household coping capacity	Analysing the ability of households to respond to the hazard	Information on the 'expandability' of particular sources of food and cash comes from community key informants and interviews with wealth groups
	→ **Projected outcome**: predicted access to food and cash for different groups and different areas, for a defined future period, relative to different thresholds		Outcome analysis is carried out by the assessment team.

75

3. Consultations with key informants at a lower level (either regional or district), and possibly some village visits, to confirm the map and clarify any outstanding issues.
4. A return to the first level to agree any changes with partners and to get a consensus on the 'final' map – although a livelihood zone map is always open to change as a result of more detailed field work.

Once livelihood zones have been defined, a baseline assessment of each zone can be carried out.

How is a baseline assessment carried out?

The phrase 'HEA field work' can usually be understood to encompass the process of baseline assessment, by which information is gathered that provides a wealth breakdown and a baseline analysis of livelihood strategies and expenditure patterns for each of the wealth groups within a livelihood zone. The most important principle of an HEA baseline assessment – and one that does not apply to assessments conducted without relation to an analytical framework – is that the practitioner is guided by a continual focus on what they need to know. It is easy, in discussions on livelihoods, to be led down tangential paths, or to spend an unbalanced amount of time on one area. An HEA assessment is an iterative learning path, with each stop along the way allowing for increased knowledge, detail and precision. Every piece of information collected in HEA field work is collected for a reason, and the fundamental simplicity of the HEA rubric allows the practitioner to understand where each piece of information fits in relation to the whole. In other words, it helps the people doing the hard graft in the field to understand the point of what they are doing at each level of inquiry.

> The fundamental simplicity of the HEA rubric allows the practitioner to understand where each piece of information they gather fits in relation to the whole.

In the field there are typically three levels at which inquiry takes place. Most HEA baseline assessments include district-level interviews. All include interviews at the community or village level, and then a further set of interviews at the household level.

1. **Interviews with district-level key informants** are necessary in order to:
    - develop or refine livelihood zones
    - choose villages considered to be typical of the livelihood zone where interviews will be conducted
    - inform them of the work and obtain agreement and clearances for working at the village level

   and, where available, to obtain information on:
    - market networks, and past events and hazards that will help construct a timeline of events for the zone, including any unusual hazard events, good production years, and conflict events
    - production and prices, which is important for building up the reference information for designing a good problem specification, and for developing a monitoring system.

   Usually, visits to the district administrative offices take around half a day.

2. **Interviews of community leaders** at the community or village level are necessary in order to:
    - gather background information on the village, including details of recent hazards and household-level responses
    - prepare a seasonal calendar of activities
    - conduct a wealth breakdown. The objectives of this are to determine:
        - the criteria by which local people define wealth groups – usually according to the ownership of land, livestock or equipment
        - the assets owned and/or accessed by different wealth groups
        - the percentage of people falling into each wealth group – commonly done using proportional piling
        - the typical household size and dynamics of each wealth group
        - other economic or social activities/characteristics typical of each group – for example, the poor may work for the wealthy and/or receive gifts from them.

   In other words, the inquiry at this level can begin to focus on how the local economy functions and how households fit into this context. Information on the crops grown and livestock raised can be put in the context of the role crops and livestock play in determining wealth, status and power; information on the natural resources available in the area is set against the questions of who takes advantage of these resources, how, and to what end.

These interviews are also important for preparing for the next stage of the inquiry at which the household-level data is obtained. Typical households from each wealth group are identified by the community key informants, who are asked to arrange interviews with representatives of these households. These community-level interviews tend to take a couple of hours, or half a day once travel and set-up time is taken into account.

3. **Focus group interviews of representatives of typical households** within each wealth group are necessary in order to gain information on:
   - access to food and cash income
   - the expandability of different sources of food and cash after a shock.

These interviews are the source of most of the information on household-level food and cash income and expenditure for the reference year. It is at this stage that the concept of the threshold is used and the adding up begins. The relative importance of each food source is calculated by converting each into calorific equivalents and expressing these as a proportion of the minimum calorific needs of the household, taken to be an average of 2,100 kcals per person per day. The cash income obtained from different sources, and patterns of expenditure, is assessed and quantified. Cross-checking is an important feature of these interviews, both during the interview and after interviews between different teams; an outline of the cross-checks made is provided in section 5.4.

> **Interviews with representatives from households typical of each wealth group are the source of most of the information on household-level food and cash income and expenditure.**

The expandability of different sources of food and cash is estimated by going through each source of food and income and quantifying the possible changes in quantity and price that the interviewees might expect in 'bad years'. Interviewees are also asked about new strategies for obtaining food or cash income that households in that wealth group may pursue. This information is supplemented and cross-checked with historical secondary data and also with simple logic. For example, if everyone tries to cope by doing more casual labouring, but there are limited employment opportunities, the wage rate will decline and there is unlikely to be any real increase in income from that activity.

Each interview is normally done with between three and five village members, each representing households of a particular wealth group. Interviews are conducted with at least three wealth groups in each village: poor, middle and better off. Given sufficient staff and time, separate interviews are conducted with groups of men and women in each wealth group. It is usually possible for one interviewer (or a two-person interviewing team) to conduct two or three interviews per day.

How is a reference year chosen?

A household economy baseline is essentially a set of reference information on what and how much people produced, bought, earned and sold and on the decisions they made regarding their livelihood strategies in a particular year.

We need to know which year this is, firstly so that we know whether the baseline data is on the high side (if the reference year was a 'good' year) or on the low side (if the reference year was a 'bad' year). But we particularly need to know in order to be able to make projections into the future using monitoring data, such as production data or prices, which in

> Identifying a 'reference year' is necessary so that monitoring data in subsequent years can be compared with that in the reference or baseline year.

HEA is defined in relation to the reference year. For example, actual or predicted crop production data for a particular year can be compared with that in the reference or baseline year and translated into a problem specification – such as 'maize production is 80% of production in the reference year'.

In most cases, the reference year chosen will be a recent year, to make recall as easy as possible, and commonly the 12 months just passed, unless an unusually large amount of food aid was distributed and unless it was a very good year. Using a bad (but not very bad) year as the reference year has certain advantages in that it already highlights the types of coping strategies people employ, and provides a good indication of just how expandable different options are. However, this is not the case if a large amount of food aid or other outside support was provided and, thus, prevented people from having to use their own coping mechanisms. Using a very good year as the reference year is usually avoided, because typical patterns of livelihood may be lost or misunderstood in a year of surplus.

Analysis of the baseline field information

One of the strengths of rapid assessment procedures is that data collected in the field can be analysed and reviewed on the spot. This is important because it allows findings to be shared between team members every day. In this way gaps in the information can be identified and followed up, new leads can be shared and appropriate avenues of further enquiry developed and pursued. It is also important that team members share their experiences with the field methodology; this helps to identify which particular approaches work best in any given setting and helps to ensure that all team members follow similar and effective procedures in the field.

There are basically three stages to the analysis:

Preliminary analysis: This includes the rapid calculations and cross-checks carried out during and immediately after each interview. These calculations are carried out by the interviewers themselves and then cross-checked by the team leader, who provides daily feedback to team members.

Interim analysis: This is carried out by the whole team together, roughly half-way through the field work. Interim analysis requires about a day and involves compiling and quickly running through the results obtained so far. The main purpose of the interim analysis is to identify key questions and issues for follow-up in the field. For example, if the first wealth breakdowns indicate an unusually high percentage of poor households in the livelihood zone, is this a fair reflection of the situation in the zone, or is it a reflection of the way the teams are posing the wealth breakdown questions? Similarly, if the amount of cash income obtained from one source (eg, firewood) is relatively high, is there an explanation for this (eg, strong demand from a neighbouring urban market), or does it require additional follow-up in the field?

Final analysis: This is carried out by the whole team together once all the interviews have been completed. It involves compiling the findings from the various interviews (district, market, community and wealth group), summarising the results and completing a series of cross-checks. The most time-consuming parts of the analysis are the compilation of the wealth breakdown and the analysis of food, income and expenditure for each of the wealth groups. Other tasks for the final analysis include finalisation of the seasonal calendar (see Figure 6).

The interim and final analyses can be carried out in one of two ways. Either the results from the various interviews can be listed and summarised on flipcharts, or the analysis can be done using the baseline storage spreadsheet (see section 4.2). This has the advantages that it requires less time and it generates a permanent record of the analysis that can be referred to in the future.

Calculations are carried out at all stages of the analysis. Figure 22 indicates when and why these calculations are done. Some of the cross-checks that are carried out during HEA data collection and analysis are shown in Table 12 in section 5.4.

Figure 22: When and why calculations are done in a baseline

1. Rapid (and possibly rough) calculations **during the interview**	**To check the:** • reasonableness • completeness • internal consistency of the interview
2. Accurate, clear and standardised calculations **after the interview**, on the interview format	**To confirm the:** • reasonableness • completeness • internal consistency of the interview **To make sure your information is:** • calculated in a standardised way • readily accessible to others on the team • made into an available record
3. Summarisation, conducted **during the interim and final analysis**, combining all interviews for an overall picture	**To build an analysis which:** • accurately represents typical households of each wealth group • is based on good quality individual interviews

Rapid rural appraisal tools

The technique most commonly used to obtain baseline HEA information is the semi-structured interview. This is an interview in which the interviewer knows exactly what questions ultimately need to be answered, but does not obtain the information through a pre-defined list of questions. Rather, they have the flexibility to pose questions in the way and order that they think will be most effective in getting that information, using simply a checklist as an aid. For example, the interviewer knows that they need details of the interviewee's income, but may not know all of the ways by which the interviewee earns money. Interviewers are also encouraged to cross-check their information and challenge the interviewee when different pieces of information contradict each other. Although they are more demanding in terms of time, training and the calibre of the interviewer, such interviews have a number of benefits over a questionnaire approach as described in Chapter 5.

A number of rapid rural appraisal techniques are commonly used in conjunction with semi-structured interviews. For example:

- **Proportional piling** can be used for wealth breakdowns (for indicating the proportion of people within each wealth group) and for gaining a broad picture of the relative importance of different food and cash sources.
- **Mapping** on the ground, using different objects to represent different activities, can help to understand the locations of key markets and the flows of goods and services in and out of the area.
- **Seasonal calendars** serve not only as a means of understanding peaks and troughs of activities, but to prompt recall and to identify gaps in information.
- **Beans** can be used to construct a historical timeline, to show good and bad years in the past by scoring them.

4.2 Storing information: HEA spreadsheets

Two types of spreadsheet have been developed by FEG to facilitate the storage, cross-checking and analysis of baseline data: the **baseline storage spreadsheet** and the **analysis spreadsheet**.

The baseline storage sheet

This is used to document and cross-check data from each interview and to facilitate post-field work analysis. It is a simple Excel spreadsheet that enables

Table 9: Advantages of the baseline storage sheet

- Encourages active checking and cross-checking of data by the field teams themselves.
- Facilitates rapid on-the-spot analysis, so that any inconsistencies or questions can be resolved by the field teams before they leave the survey area.
- Minimises data entry errors, while at the same time speeding up the processing of basic field data.
- Provides a permanent record of individual interview results and the analyses completed by the field teams, so that these can be checked by a supervisor at a later date.

field teams to enter, check and analyse individual interview data in the field. It is also the basic tool that field teams use to analyse and summarise field data during the interim and final data analysis sessions.

The spreadsheet performs a number of calculations that form the basis of key household economy cross-checks:

- **Calculation of total food access**: If this is very much below 100% of minimum food energy needs, and people clearly did not starve in the reference year, then more questions need to be asked and clarification obtained.
- **Calculation and comparison of total cash income and expenditure**: If these are very different, then further follow-up is required to resolve the apparent inconsistency.
- **Calculation of rates of off-take for each type of livestock** (ie, the percentage of the herd sold and slaughtered in the reference year): This can be compared with a set of reference values; again, any major deviation signals the need for further follow-up in the field.
- **A cross-check on labour payments**: This determines whether the amount of money reportedly earned by poorer wealth groups roughly balances with the amount that the better off report paying for labour.
- **A cross-check on agricultural productivity**: This compares the production per unit area obtained by different wealth groups, to check that trends are consistent across wealth groups (and are consistent with reported rates of input use, etc).

• THE HOUSEHOLD ECONOMY APPROACH

The analysis spreadsheets

The analysis spreadsheets are used for the outcome analysis, to determine how baseline access to food and income will be affected by particular hazards. There are two types of analysis spreadsheet:
- the **single zone spreadsheet**, used to prepare scenarios for a single livelihood zone
- the **integrated spreadsheet**, used for the analysis of larger geographical areas of up to 12 livelihood zones.

All the analysis spreadsheets are linked to the baseline storage sheets, and read the baseline data from these sheets.

The analysis spreadsheets make the process of outcome analysis a great deal quicker and easier than when done with pen and paper. Hazard information, translated into a percentage change of each source of food and cash income in the baseline, is entered into the analysis spreadsheet in a standard format. The spreadsheet then combines this information with household economy baseline data to project likely future access to food and non-food goods and services at household level.

Where HEA is used within a rural monitoring system, an outcome analysis typically covers a 12-month period, beginning with the main harvest (in an agricultural setting), or the main season rains (in a pastoral setting). An initial analysis will normally be prepared immediately after the harvest or after the rains, projecting access for the next 12 months, with updates prepared at various times during the remainder of the year (eg, after a subsidiary harvest or secondary rainy season). In many cases it will be useful to prepare a preliminary analysis before any assessment field work is undertaken, using whatever information is available to hand, and then to re-run the analysis once the field work has been completed. This type of preliminary analysis can help identify gaps in the available data, which in turn helps with the planning of the field work.

4.3 Is HEA always done in the same way?

The range of circumstances in which HEA has been used has led to methodological adaptations that reflect differences in context, purpose, geographical access and security, and the time, staff and funding available. Two variants of HEA, 'rapid' and 'disaggregated', are described below.

Rapid variants of HEA

There are times when it will not be possible to do a full HEA assessment, and there is a need for a rapid assessment of the situation to inform interventions. Most commonly, this occurs after a rapid-onset disaster, or where there is limited access to the focus population (for example, in an insecure environment), or where a provisional assessment is needed to determine whether it is worthwhile carrying out a more detailed assessment. Unfortunately, a rapid assessment may also have to be carried out when the response to slow-onset disasters, such as drought, has not been timely and actors scramble to react to the resulting crisis.

HEA has been adapted to these circumstances in a variety of ways. At a global level, rapid HEA assessments have been carried out in recent years, after the 2004 tsunami in Asia, the 2005 earthquake in Kashmir, and the 2006 conflict in Lebanon. Within southern Africa, examples include assessing the effects of the floods in Mozambique in 2000, the impact of the land reform programme in Zimbabwe in 2001/02, and the impact of the 2002 drought in Malawi. The assessments can provide information for emergency responses, and can also be important, from an advocacy perspective, for raising awareness of the nature of problems and giving broad guidance on types of interventions that might be appropriate.

The key challenge in carrying out rapid assessments is to find the optimal trade-off between the need for faster results and the need to maintain the quality and reliability of the information collected. How this balance is achieved varies from context to context and according to the users' needs. This has meant that there is no single 'rapid HEA' model. However, there are some key principles to ensuring quality in rapid assessments:

- **The more rapid the assessment, the more skilled and experienced** the assessment team needs to be. The team needs to be aware of the implications of simplifying the classic HEA assessment, and should be able to bring their experience to bear in quickly interpreting and understanding data collected.
- Some time is saved by **keeping the number of interviews down** to between four and six for each wealth group, and/or focusing only on those groups known to be worst affected. However, more time is often saved by **collecting less detail** within each interview. 'Rapid HEAs' often involve less quantification than full HEA assessments. For example, the level of detail

on expenditure is often reduced, while very minor sources of food and income may not be quantified.
- In rapid assessments, there is an even greater need to be disciplined in **focusing only on the specified research needs**, whether that be determining food aid needs, identifying how to restore lost sources of income, or simply explaining in a narrative form how livelihoods have been changed by a specific event.
- **Scenario-based analyses** can be particularly useful. Knowing that 'quick and dirty' assessments will be less comprehensive and/or the situation may simply be more unpredictable, it is often advisable to present alternative scenarios (best case, worst case) and recommendations for each.

The methods used in rapid assessments can vary significantly. Some rely heavily on key informant interviews, some use focus groups but with less detail, some use large numbers of short individual household interviews, and some have used a detailed case-study approach with a small number of households or a small sample of villages. Combinations of these have also been used. In a crisis situation where life-saving interventions are necessary, or where the assessment needs to cover a wide area, less detailed interviews with a relatively large sample are preferable.

Disaggregated variants of HEA

A four-way wealth breakdown (very poor, poor, middle and better off) has been found to give a sufficiently detailed picture of the different livelihood patterns within a population for many purposes, including early warning, assessing emergency and post-emergency needs and for guiding poverty reduction strategies (see Chapter 3). It can also provide useful information in terms of social protection guidance, as illustrated in section 3.5.

But social protection planners also require data that relates to households defined in all sorts of other ways: households with children, pensioner- or female-headed households, or those with orphans or people affected by HIV and AIDS. They need to be able to compare the effectiveness of different social protection instruments in supporting different kinds of households in different ways. Can HEA offer an analysis that is sufficiently disaggregated to be useful for these purposes?

The answer is that the HEA framework can be applied at the level of disaggregation required for the purpose, using the information-collection and sampling tools that are most appropriate. While the four-way wealth breakdown has been found to work for the purposes of many HEA analyses, it is not a division that, on its own, meets every information need. Determining ways of helping the poorest will commonly require paying more attention to particular subgroups within the 'poor' category. In Singida, Tanzania, and in Tigray, Ethiopia, poor female-headed households – a highly labour-constrained subset of the 'poor' group – have been the subject of separate inquiry and have been investigated using purposive sampling (see section 3.4). Interviews with *individual* households have also been used in conjunction with other methods to gain a deeper understanding of the extremely poor and of the impact on households of chronic illness.[27] Such in-depth micro-studies can be very effective in complementing existing national datasets such as household budget surveys, and in highlighting ways of helping the very poor households whom NGOs and governments may see as a priority.

This approach works well for investigating a subset of a wealth group, or any group in which there is relatively little variation in patterns of access. But for some groups of interest, there is often a great deal of variation. The broad category of 'HIV/AIDS-affected' can include families with someone who is chronically ill, families who have recently lost an income-earner, or families who have taken in an orphaned child. The constraints and opportunities of households in each of these categories will be very different; and there will also be differences within each category according to differences in wealth. For the analysis of such groups, it becomes necessary to disaggregate further (commonly by wealth) so that the group is sufficiently homogeneous for the analysis to yield meaningful results.

When HEA assessments are done using focus group interviews, it is necessary simply to ensure that these additional groups are purposively sampled. This does require extra time, but the HEA framework itself is not a hindrance in this regard. The problem with such purposive sampling is that such groups have to be predetermined, and the analyst does not have the flexibility to carry out analyses of other groups or of households with other, quite different, characteristics after the inquiry has finished. Randomly sampled household economy surveys of individual households may be appropriate in cases where analyses need to be conducted according to a very wide range of different household characteristics. However, such disaggregation does require a large sample if it is to be valid.

Finally, HEA wealth group data has been used to generate an income profile across the population (see Figure 23).[28] This was done by interpolating differences within wealth groups using the lower and upper points in the range of income data collected for each wealth group – ie, it used the simplifying assumption that income levels were evenly distributed within the range identified for each wealth group. The resulting income distribution can be used for estimating the number of people falling below a certain standard of living threshold, and for monitoring changes in poverty levels as a result of economic shocks such as a price rise (see Figure 23).

Figure 23: Interpolating income differences within wealth groups – Hargeisa, 2003

In an assessment of Hargeisa, Somaliland in 2003, four wealth groups were identified. Using the range of income for each wealth group, income data was converted into deciles to produce the income distribution shown here. This could be used to determine the number of people falling below a certain threshold and how that would be affected by inflation.

Income profile of urban population, Hargeisa

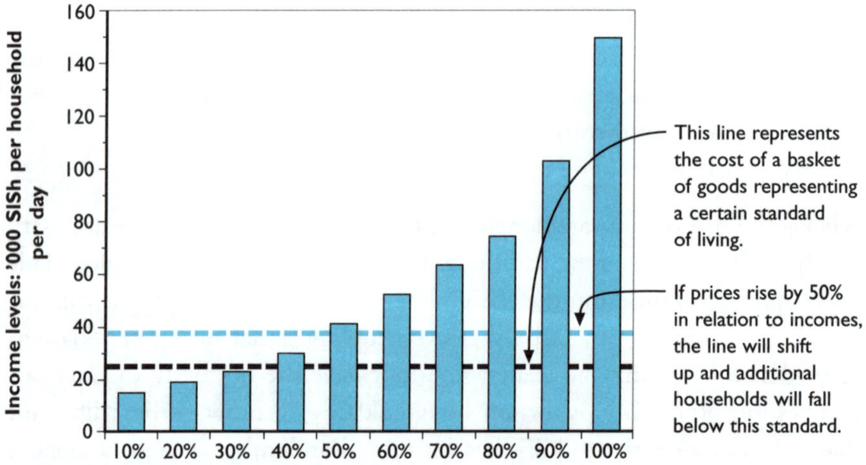
Income levels: '000 SlSh per household per day
160
140
120
100
80
60
40
20
0
10%
20%
30%
40%
50%
60%
70%
80%
90%
100%
This line represents the cost of a basket of goods representing a certain standard of living.
If prices rise by 50% in relation to incomes, the line will shift up and additional households will fall below this standard.

Source: King with Mohamed and Addou (2003)

The Individual Household Model (IHM)[29]

A more formalised disaggregated variant of HEA is the Individual Household Model (IHM). IHM was developed as a tool for looking at poverty and livelihoods issues on the basis that the collection and analysis of data from individual households can offer a finer distinction between different types of household (for example, on the basis of household demographic characteristics) and the opportunity for forms of analysis that cannot be carried out in 'classic' HEA. IHM uses the standard HEA analytical framework but its field methods and data set are somewhat different. Information in the field is gathered via semi-structured interviews with individual households, rather than with groups of households representative of a wealth group. The sample either includes all households in the survey site, or is based on statistical sampling techniques, and demographic data tends to be collected during interviews as well as standard household economy data. IHM has, to date, been carried out at a very local level, with survey sites of one or two villages.

Because data is collected on individual households, IHM enables an analysis to be made of the relationships between poverty and particular household characteristics (for example, between poverty and households with orphans or grandparent-headed households). It also enables an analysis of the impact of change within the household – for example, as a result of illness or disability. An IHM study of a community in Swaziland, for example, aimed to identify the main factors affecting income levels for HIV-affected and non-HIV-affected households. By looking at households with orphans and at the mortality in the village, the study enabled an estimate to be made of the decline in relative disposable income as a result of the loss of income due to HIV mortality and as a result of taking in orphans, household by household and collectively as a community. Because IHM studies focus on limited geographical areas, they also have the potential to go into more detail than classic HEA.

Other uses of IHM to date have been to understand the relationship between wealth and children's nutritional status (Bangladesh), to get a detailed understanding of the poorest and destitute households in a community (Tanzania), to model the impact of changes in coffee prices on the disposable income of communities in Uganda and Ethiopia, and to model the impact of different social protection policies (Zambia). The method continues to be developed.

4.4 What does HEA require in terms of resources?

Human resources

The table opposite outlines the resources required for a livelihood zoning exercise and for conducting a baseline assessment.

The exact time required varies according to factors such as the geographical spread of the area covered, prior knowledge of and existing information about the area, and the extent of organisational support in the field (for example, ongoing projects can provide useful information as well as access to knowledgeable key informants).

What size of sample is used in an HEA baseline assessment?

Although there are no hard and fast rules about sample frame and sample size, there is a body of experience that can provide some guidance. The most important factor to consider is the number of interviews undertaken with each wealth group. Practical experience indicates that for a comprehensive baseline assessment across several livelihood zones – for the purposes of a national early warning or vulnerability analysis system, for example – 8–12 interviews should be completed for each wealth group per livelihood zone. This will normally entail visiting 8–12 villages per zone. It is usually desirable for at least two interviewers to work together (to allow for the minimum of triangulation between different investigators), and experience has shown that a two-person team can do a maximum of two household representative interviews in one village in one day. Thus, with eight villages, it will take four teams approximately six days to complete both the community leader and household representative interviews. Additional time is required for interviews at higher administrative levels (1–2 days), for analysis (2–3 days in the field), and for travel, so it is not unreasonable to expect a comprehensive assessment of one livelihood zone to be completed within 10–14 days, depending upon local circumstances on the ground.

More interviews can be carried out, given sufficient time and resources, and where the geographical area to be covered is smaller. For baselines carried out to inform more **localised project work**, the coverage of a smaller geographical area may be offset by the need to obtain more disaggregated data (for example, on sub-groups of the poor), or to spend more time doing separate interviews with men and women.

Table 10: Human resources required for livelihood zoning and baseline assessment on a regional or national level

Step	Human resources	Time
Livelihood zoning		
1. Review of secondary information and preliminary discussions	1 zoning director 1 local counterpart	2 days
2. Workshop	1 zoning director 1 local counterpart Max. 20 workshop participants 1 facilitator per 10 participants	2–3 days
3. Follow-up at lower administrative levels (region or district)	1 zoning director 1 local counterpart	2–5 days
4. Final consultation	1 zoning director 1 local counterpart	0.5 day
5. Production of final outputs	Depends on availability of digitised mapping data and number of zones	
6. Field check (per zone)	Field teams check zone boundaries during baseline field work	c.1 hour within each district-level interview
Baseline assessment		
1. Secondary literature review	1 survey director 1 local counterpart	1 week
2. Training	Max. 20 participants 2 facilitators per 10 participants	1 week
3. Field work and interim analysis (per zone)	4 x 2-person teams	2 weeks
4. Final analysis (all zones)	All teams together	1 week
5. Report writing	Team leaders	Around 3 days per livelihood zone plus 5 days for the national overview

For the preparation of more **rapid baselines**, usually associated with periodic emergency needs assessments, a smaller number of interviews can be conducted and villages visited; perhaps half the number suggested above. Larger teams can also allow the work to proceed more rapidly. A team of four people could be expected to cover three livelihood zones in a rapid assessment in just over three weeks, including interviews at various administrative levels and the interim and final analyses. If the team members are inexperienced in the approach, however, additional time for training at the start of the assessment and for analysis would have to be added.

What other resources are needed?

Other resources include:
- transport to the region and in the field
- accommodation for international and national consultants
- expenses and per diems for international and national staff
- stationery, paper and printing.

This will vary from country to country.

5 Is HEA reliable?

5.1 Why is HEA information collected through rapid appraisal?

Rapid appraisal methods and sample surveys have different strengths, based on certain key features. The key features of rapid appraisal are that information and analysis are generated relatively quickly, and that the approach is open-ended and semi-structured. Sample surveys are generally valued for the level of detail in the data collected, its precision and its representativeness. Rapid appraisal typically involves interviews with groups of people, selected because they are thought either to have specialist knowledge or to be in some way representative of a defined group. Most sample surveys focus on the household level, collecting data using a standardised questionnaire from a carefully selected and (usually) large number of households.

Given these differences, the reasons why HEA data has to date been collected through rapid appraisal are twofold. First, there are the practical reasons. HEA aims to provide decision-makers with the information they require, within the time-frame

> In HEA, data collection and analysis are continuous processes undertaken throughout the field work.

they need it, with enough rigour and validity to inspire action. Information and analysis that feed into humanitarian decision-making are nearly always needed quickly and with limited resources, and rapid appraisal has proved to be a fast and relatively inexpensive way of gathering reliable data on livelihoods. In a rapid appraisal, data collection and analysis are continuous processes undertaken throughout the field work, and a rapid appraisal team is typically able to present its main findings and conclusions shortly after completing the field work. Sample surveys tend to take longer. Prior to the field work, the construction of the sample frames required for a statistically valid analysis may take some time, especially when the required information (lists of villages or population data, for example) is incomplete, inaccurate or out of date. Cleaning and processing of field data may also be time-consuming, with the result that sample survey results are rarely available until at least a month (and often much longer) after the completion of the field work.

Rapid appraisals tend also to be less costly than sample surveys, in which the larger sample size tends to push up both the transport and staff costs. However, while fewer people are involved in a rapid appraisal, their unit cost tends to be higher because this type of assessment requires a higher calibre of field staff. In HEA, the baseline analysis is to a great extent carried out in the field by the field workers themselves, who, therefore, require appropriate training beforehand.

But leaving aside the question of resources and timeliness, which method is thought to generate the better quality information? It is difficult to argue that one approach is consistently better than another – to some extent they serve different purposes, they have different requirements in terms of time, staff and technical input, and – a key factor – both types of assessment can be well or badly done. But the second reason why HEA data tends to be collected through rapid appraisal lies in the quality control measures that such methods allow, linked largely to the opportunity to clarify, discuss, cross-check and triangulate. The investigator can check items of reported information against others (reported access to food against minimum food needs; reported income against expenditure), and is trained to challenge respondents when parts of the account contradict each other, until a logical and internally consistent picture is constructed of how people survive through the year. The advantages of an iterative, semi-structured method have particular weight in a system-based approach such as HEA that seeks to construct a picture of 'how things work', rather than to compile a set of statistics.

> The advantages of an iterative, semi-structured method have particular weight in a system-based approach such as HEA that seeks to construct a picture of 'how things work'.

This is not to say that quality control measures cannot be implemented in sample surveys. But given the requirements in terms of training, the calibre of staff and the time needed for each interview, it does mean that it is difficult to obtain the number of HEA interviews necessary for statistical purposes. The resource limits that are invariably placed on assessments mean that, in reality, a choice has to be made between a high volume of lower-quality data and a small volume of higher-quality data. Rapid appraisal methods tend to put more weight on the quality of each interview, rather than on the number of interviews per se, and err towards the second option. The question then becomes: how representative is the information of the group or population as a whole?

> Information quality is determined by a number of factors; one of which is sampling – which determines the ability to conduct standard statistical analyses and measure the precision of the data.

5.2 Representativeness: questions of sampling

Obtaining a result that is representative of a given group or population as a whole presents a major challenge in any type of assessment, as it is never feasible to conduct interviews in every household or village. Some form of sampling is therefore required, which will provide a result that is representative of the population and not biased in any way – for example, towards villages that are nearer to a road. In random or probability sampling, every sample unit, such as the household or village, has a known chance of being selected and a sample size can be calculated on the basis of a known sampling error. Such methods include two-stage cluster sampling, stratified sampling or simple random sampling, and are commonly used in household sample surveys. They give the best chance of obtaining a sample that is truly representative, provided that accurate data is available on both sample locations and populations. If this information is not available, or is incomplete or inaccurate or out of date (as is often the case), then the representativeness of the sample is adversely affected.

In **purposive** sampling, sample units are selected on the basis of their known characteristics, these being thought to make them representative of the group as a whole. In an HEA assessment, representativeness is ensured through the purposive sampling of areas and groups considered to be relatively homogeneous in terms of livelihood. People are grouped together who share common livelihood patterns, firstly through the delineation of livelihood zones (areas within which people share similar options for obtaining food and income), and secondly through disaggregation into wealth groups (within which people share similar strategies for obtaining food and income). In consultation with key informants, villages considered to be typical of the livelihood zone, and within these villages men and women from households considered to be typical of particular wealth groups, are selected. Techniques for minimising bias in these selection processes are built into HEA's quality control; teams are trained to carefully present

> In an **HEA** assessment, **representativeness is ensured through the purposive sampling of areas and groups considered to be relatively homogeneous in terms of livelihood.**

the purpose of their visit and to explain clearly the nature of the wealth groups and the representatives with whom they wish to speak. These representatives are interviewed until the investigator judges that a reasonably consistent picture has emerged for that group. Experience with HEA has been that, through the process of grouping like with like, this can often be achieved with a rather smaller sample size than in the case of a survey based on a form of random sampling.

Guidance on the sample size, staffing and time requirements for a baseline assessment is given in section 4.4 above.

5.3 Can key informants and focus groups provide useful quantitative data?

Assessing the relative importance of different activities involves asking questions of 'how much': how much does a typical family in a particular wealth group normally produce? How many livestock does that typical family sell in a year? These are questions that are usually tackled, if at all, by household surveys. But experience has shown that, with appropriate selection of informants and proper cross-checking, rapid appraisal can be used to generate quantitative as well as qualitative data. Certainly the quantitative data is not of the measured or objective kind; for example, an investigator may ask a village key informant how many sacks an average household harvested, but they cannot count those sacks. But in truth this is also the case with most food security data collected via sample surveys, where the number of sacks harvested is also reported, not counted. Survey data is thus as susceptible to inaccurate reporting by interviewees as any other; the difference is that the sample enables a statistical analysis to be made of the precision of the data collected.

The use of rapid appraisal techniques to collect quantitative HEA data has the advantage that it allows for cross-checking within and between interviews so that the information is internally consistent and contributes to a picture in which 'things add up' both quantitatively and logically. This is a key factor in minimising the errors arising from the subjectivity of responses or the ambiguity of questions, and is described in section 5.4 below. With such cross-checking, experience has shown that the judgement of informants on quantitative questions – such as the typical livestock holding of an area, or the proportion of people in villages belonging to different wealth categories – deserves the same confidence that we instinctively give to their judgement on qualitative questions such as the types and uses of livestock.

> In sample surveys, as in rapid appraisal, most food security data is reported, not measured, and so open to a degree of subjective judgement.

5.4 Rigour, verification and bias

One of the advantages of sample survey methodology is that standard statistical analyses can be used to estimate how precise the data is; that is, to estimate whether the same result would be obtained if the survey were repeated and to make statistically valid comparisons between the results from different population groups. Precision is not, however, the same thing as accuracy. Suppose that household interviewees consistently underestimate their crop production by 10–30%, so that the average result obtained in repeated surveys is eight sacks per household rather than ten, the true or accurate figure. In this case, the result (eight sacks) is inaccurate (because the true figure is ten sacks) but it is precise (because the same result would be obtained in a repeat survey).

It is very difficult to determine accuracy with respect to data on food security, but there are two important and related advantages to HEA in this respect. The first is that in the kinds of (especially rural) economy in which HEA inquiries are usually carried out, there is quite a limited range of possible items to record: few types of food, few sources of food, few places of purchase; few kinds of cash expenditure, and few kinds of income beyond the farm. Tied to this, the second advantage is that there is a simple arithmetical test of whether the information is making sense: it actually has to *add up*. An analysis of food income lends itself to such testing, since there is a minimum 'food income' below which year-on-year survival is impossible. For instance, if people have clearly not starved within the last 12 months, however disadvantaged they may be in many ways, but the information they are giving suggests household food access significantly below the 2,100 kcals per person per day threshold, then more questions need to be asked and clarification obtained.

In HEA interviews, the same principle applies to information on income, which can be cross-checked with stated expenditure[30] and with the observed standard of living; and with information on particular household strategies, which must correspond with the characteristics of the local economy. For example, information on the type and length of work the better off can offer to the poor, and the wage rates they offer, have to be reconciled with a statement of the type: 'a typical poor farmer depends for four months of the year on the casual employment offered by neighbouring farmers'.

Cross-checking of information within interviews and between informants is extremely important in HEA and is a key aspect of information-gathering in the field (see Table 11 for more examples). It is formalised in the baseline storage spreadsheet, which is used regularly during field work (see section 4.2 above). Importantly, the approach allows the field worker to appreciate and follow up *on the spot* answers that seem to be an underestimate. In this way, the baseline analysis is not conducted outside the context in which the information is collected, but rather it is carried out by the field workers themselves. Such cross-checking is also possible (and is as necessary) with the sample survey approach; but since it is best done and followed up in the field, and requires training and a relatively high calibre of staff, it tends not to be a feature of questionnaire-based sample surveys.

> In HEA, the baseline analysis is not conducted outside the context in which the information is collected, but rather it is carried out by the field workers themselves.

There is, however, a strict limit to the verification of this type of information. Despite one's best efforts, bias can never be eliminated from reported information, whether gained from questionnaire surveys or by rapid rural appraisal methods. Respondents know they are talking to people involved in humanitarian assistance in some way, and it is natural to want to give a picture in which their need for assistance is evident. The best one can do is to be aware of and manage potential bias by being sensitive regarding the person to whom you are talking, being clear about the geographical area to which they are referring (spatial bias), including a seasonal perspective (seasonal bias), and making sure that the poor and women are well represented, at least as subjects of the inquiry (wealth, influence and male bias).

> **Checking for internal consistency is important in minimising bias: providing a false picture that is complete *and* consistent is extremely difficult to do.**

In reality, most HEA practitioners would perhaps say that one's own conviction of having found something like the truth, and being able to demonstrate the reasons for this, is something like a non-statistical 'test of confidence'. Strict adherence to statistical procedures is essential in many fields of inquiry, but given the limitations and costs it imposes, it can actually be an obstacle to initiatives to gain an understanding of rural livelihoods and food security.

Table 11: Cross-checks carried out on HEA information to ensure quality control

Within an interview	• Are households consuming close to 2,100 kcals per person? • Do income and expenditure match? • Ask the same question a number of different ways (How much did you harvest? How long did it last? How much was eaten every month during that time?) • Check the timing of activities: can all of those things be done with the time and labour available? • Check the timing of food and income flows; are we accounting for all times of the year?
Between interviews	• Are wealth groups and key informants giving the same picture? • Are the same wealth groups giving the same picture? • Data such as rainfall, yields, prices and wage rates should not vary very much within the same zone and time period.

continued overleaf

Table 12 *continued*

Between primary and secondary data	Likely to be some differences here as secondary data is rarely exactly comparable to primary data... ...Nonetheless, bear in mind possible biases in primary data, and, with secondary data, possible limitations of the methodology.
Between reported and observed information	• Always keep your eyes open! Observe crops in fields, grain stores, livestock condition, physical condition of people, etc. • Observe what food people are preparing. • See who is doing what.
Triangulation	Means looking at things from different perspectives: • team composition (gender, multi-disciplinary, knowledge of area) • units of observation (age, gender, status, wealth, ethnicity, professions/activities) • tools and techniques.
Common pitfalls	• Clarify year and wealth group under discussion. • Check units of measurement being used. • Methods of storage/consumption: (milled/threshed, etc). • Method of consumption ('green' crops). • Utilisation of food: don't assume it is all consumed.

6 Looking forward and outward: links to other approaches and issues

HEA differs from other approaches to vulnerability or livelihood analysis in both the structure of its framework and in the methods typically used for collecting information. Acknowledging these differences helps to highlight areas of complementarity, which allow different tools to add value to each other when used together. The contrasting perspectives offered by different approaches can contribute to a more rounded analysis of livelihoods and vulnerability, and a fuller understanding of the constraints people face in accessing basic services and getting their basic needs met. In addition, the constant evolution of vulnerability assessment methods, including HEA, means that different methods can benefit from the experience of others. The links between HEA and different approaches that can facilitate this are described in section 6.1 below.

In the same way, there are obvious points of connection and areas of overlap between HEA and other subject areas such as nutrition, market analysis and political economy analysis. It is worth pointing out here that HEA is not an analytical tool that is relevant for all purposes and for all areas of inquiry. It was designed for a certain purpose and its central livelihood focus means that it has been put to a range of uses and has relevance to a number of other fields. But there are limits to what HEA can do and what its analysis can cover. In describing how HEA links with other areas of analysis (see section 6.2), we hope that these limits will be clarified and that ways in which different areas of inquiry can complement and add value to each other can be developed.

> Acknowledging the differences between methodologies helps to identify ways they can add value to each other.

Finally, this section outlines how HEA can contribute to certain issues that are a challenge for all frameworks designed for the analysis of poverty, vulnerability and livelihoods. These include distinguishing between chronic and transitory food insecurity, comparing levels of poverty across geographical areas, and looking at the needs of specific groups, such as HIV-affected households and children (section 6.3).

6.1 How HEA links to other approaches and systems

HEA and other approaches to vulnerability analysis

'Vulnerability' is a term used in different ways. Some approaches define vulnerability in terms of an outcome, such as food insecurity, hunger or poverty, with 'the vulnerable' taken to be the most food insecure, or the poorest, or those with the fewest assets. In other approaches, including HEA, vulnerability means something quite different; it refers to how susceptible a household or population group is to a particular hazard that might result in an outcome such as food insecurity or hunger. In these terms, there is no general or absolute state of vulnerability; people can only be vulnerable *to something*. For example, households that depend on remittances from South Africa may not be vulnerable to drought, but may be vulnerable to inflation, since they rely on the market for access to food. How a household obtains access to food and cash thus determines which shocks or hazards will affect it, and to what degree – that is, how vulnerable it is to specific hazards. Understanding what different methods mean by 'vulnerability' is important because it underlies the approach taken in each case.

In considering different approaches to vulnerability analysis, it is worth emphasising that the usefulness of any survey or piece of research relates to its content and quality. Does the inquiry answer the questions of concern to the user? And can the user trust that the data has been collected in a way that ensures it is representative of the population it claims to describe, and that the method used will produce robust and accurate information? Quality is not inherent in the method chosen for research, but rather is determined by how the

> Quality is not inherent in the method chosen for research, but rather is determined by how the research is carried out in practice.

research is carried out in practice and what it is used for. In practice, of course, the choice of framework or method does not hinge wholly on issues of content and quality; practical considerations of time, geographical coverage, money and staff availability tend to be at least as important.

'Snapshots' vs annual accounting of food security and vulnerability

Most approaches to vulnerability analysis are based on the collection of some combination of information on food consumption, income and spending, gathered either for a particular point in time, such as the previous seven days (to create a 'snapshot'), or over a longer period, usually a full year (described as 'annual accounting'), as is typically done in HEA. Just as HEA assessments commonly use rapid appraisal methods, so snapshot or annual accounting assessments are typically carried out using household questionnaire surveys.

Snapshots potentially provide more accurate information than annual accounting assessments because of the shorter recall period. But they are limited in that often they do not take account of seasonal factors and inter-annual differences and, thus, the information for that point in time is hard to contextualise: are things improving or declining, and is the situation normal or unusual for that time of year? Thus, unless they are repeated frequently to enable comparison over time, this makes them less useful for early warning and making predictions of how things will change. Examples of surveys that are predominantly 'snapshot' in their nature include the World Food Programme's (WFP's) Comprehensive Food Security and Vulnerability Assessments (CFSVAs) and many national household budget surveys or income and expenditure surveys.

Annual accounting of food, income and expenditure in a household survey is more demanding than getting snapshot information. It can be difficult to recall accurately things that happened many months previously. However, a well-designed method would facilitate recall by including opportunities for cross-checking information, and by asking questions in ways that are easier for respondents to answer. Some Vulnerability Assessment Committee (VAC) assessments have used this approach (such as in Zimbabwe in 2003/04), while others use a combination of 'snapshot' indicators and more or less comprehensive accounting of the household economy within a single survey, such as that carried out by the Mozambique VAC in 2005/06, and the Malawi Integrated Household Survey 2 of 2004.

HEA and other approaches can add value to each other in that different methods of information collection, and different types of information, can be highly complementary. For example, an HEA assessment carried out prior to a household survey can be useful for designing the survey questionnaire and indicating key questions to include. Similarly, HEA assessments can complement 'snapshot' surveys by providing the contextual, seasonal or narrative background against which the survey data can be interpreted. It is less efficient to use HEA assessments and other annual accounting surveys together, as the added benefits are mainly related to cross-checking results and possibly better coverage in HEA of informal income sources. Where an annual accounting survey has national coverage, an HEA assessment may usefully complement it by providing a more detailed description of a smaller geographical area.

It may also be useful to carry out an HEA assessment or qualitative livelihoods research after either a 'snapshot' or annual accounting household survey to investigate and explain anomalous or unexpected findings.

Qualitative livelihoods research

The two most common types of qualitative livelihoods assessments are those based on the Sustainable Livelihoods Framework (SLF), often carried out by NGOs such as Oxfam and CARE, and Participatory Poverty Appraisals (PPAs), carried out by the World Bank. Such research typically covers a broad range of issues relating to livelihoods and vulnerability, and the information collected can be very rich and useful in understanding livelihoods patterns and the root causes of poverty. Results are not quantified, however, which can be a constraint in determining the relative importance of different issues and the scale of responses required.

In practice, HEAs typically cover a large subset of the issues investigated in qualitative livelihoods assessments, but add a quantitative aspect. Rather than carry out two separate surveys, it may be more useful to budget additional time in an HEA assessment to provide better coverage of the full range of issues, if the research question requires this.

HEA and the Sustainable Livelihoods Framework

The SLF is an analytical framework that helps us to understand how assets, institutions and processes combine to enable households to make a living. The framework has five broad components:

6 LOOKING FORWARD AND OUTWARD: LINKS TO OTHER APPROACHES AND ISSUES

- **Assets or capitals**: different assets can contribute to making a living – human, financial, physical, natural, social and – in some variants of the SLF – political.
- **Policies, institutions and processes**: these influence and mediate the ways that households can use the assets that are available to them.
- **The vulnerability context**: this describes the external environment in which people exist but which they cannot control, and refers to how long-term trends, seasonality and natural and man-made shocks can affect livelihoods.
- **Livelihood strategies**: on the basis of the interaction of the above three sets of factors, households are able to carry out different livelihood strategies, such as farming, employment or trading.
- **Livelihood outcomes**: these refer to how successful the livelihood strategies have been in ensuring access to food or income or other measures of welfare.

Although HEA was developed before and independently of the SLF, the two share many common elements. HEA explicitly describes livelihood strategies and outcomes through an analysis of sources of food and income and of expenditure patterns. The wealth breakdown in HEA looks at the assets available to the households, and this can be expressed in terms of the five types of assets or capitals in the SLF. In practice, however, most HEA assessments have not looked in detail at the 'quality' of human capital (that is, the education or skills and health status of different wealth groups), but have focused more on the quantity of labour typically available in different wealth groups.

In HEA, the vulnerability context is expressed in terms of a problem specification for a current year and more broadly as a description in the baseline report of the different shocks to which households are vulnerable. HEA assessments do not usually include an explicit analysis of policies, institutions and processes, and this is an area that could be strengthened. Currently, it is common within HEA to describe aspects of key policies, institutions and processes where they help explain the wealth breakdown or different aspects of access to food and income or expenditure patterns.

Given their respective roots as tools for emergency assessments and for more development-oriented planning, HEA assessments have tended to focus on livelihood strategies and outcomes, while SLF assessments have focused more on understanding the factors underlying those strategies and outcomes. However, while there may be time and resource issues to consider, there is no methodological reason why greater emphasis could not be placed on understanding all types of capitals and policies, institutions and processes in HEA interviews, if that is what is required from the research question. Alternatively, additional specialised tools could be combined with HEA to ensure adequate coverage of all aspects of livelihoods, such as the 'social relations framework', for understanding power and social dynamics.

Meanwhile, adding an element of quantification to descriptions of livelihood strategies and outcomes means that decision-makers can understand the relative importance to different groups of different ways of getting food and income, and can see and compare absolute levels of food insecurity and poverty. This makes HEA a very useful tool for operationalising the Sustainable Livelihoods Framework.

> As an approach that provides a quantified view of livelihoods and a practical method for information collection, HEA is a useful tool for operationalising the Sustainable Livelihoods Framework.

HEA and the Integrated Phase Classification

The Integrated Food Security and Humanitarian Phase Classification (IPC) is a system for defining the severity of a situation, based on a wide range of indicators of the impact of a hazard event on human health and welfare (such as mortality rate and nutritional status). The IPC is intended as a tool to build consensus about the severity of a humanitarian problem. The classification places a country along a scale from 'generally food secure' to 'famine/humanitarian catastrophe'. While the system was developed originally by FAO in Somalia, the classification is intended to be internationally comparable, and, as such, is particularly attractive to donors as an aid to prioritising resource allocation between and within countries.

The IPC is a classification scheme. It is not a method of assessment and does not generate estimates of beneficiary numbers or amounts of assistance. It gives broad guidance on the type of assistance that is appropriate in each phase, but cannot on its own give detailed information on locally appropriate responses. The IPC relies on existing information sources to provide the data needed to

6 LOOKING FORWARD AND OUTWARD: LINKS TO OTHER APPROACHES AND ISSUES

classify the situation – a process described as 'meta-analysis'. Within these potentially disparate sources of information, analysts look for a convergence of evidence pointing towards a particular phase, rather than relying on strict thresholds. IPC does not prescribe methods of collecting information. However, the ability of IPC to go beyond simply classifying the situation and to predict how the situation will develop, and what precise responses will be appropriate, depends on the methods used for collecting the reference information.

> The IPC relies on existing information sources to provide the data needed to classify a situation. Its ability to predict how a situation will develop, therefore, depends on the methods used to collect and analyse the reference information.

HEA complements the IPC well, and, indeed, was a major component of the food security information system in Somalia that underpinned the IPC's development there. HEA normally collects information on a number of the key reference outcomes used in the IPC, such as food access, livelihood assets, coping strategies and hazards. But in addition to supplying information to determine the phase that a particular area is currently in, HEA can further complement the IPC by (1) estimating numbers of people in need, types and amounts of assistance required, and the time frame for delivering the assistance; and (2) predicting future phases. The ability to predict how the situation will develop is a particular advantage of HEA over other systems for vulnerability assessment (see 'HEA and other approaches to vulnerability analysis' earlier in this section for more on this), and would further enhance the usefulness of the IPC to decision-makers at national and international level.

6.2 How HEA links to other areas of inquiry

HEA and nutrition

Food security assessments and nutrition surveys and analyses are frequently carried out independently of one another, but the information provided by one can be very useful to the other. Most obviously, a HEA assessment tells us about the access of different wealth groups to their minimum energy needs. However, energy is only one component of an adequate diet, and, indeed, food

• THE HOUSEHOLD ECONOMY APPROACH

insecurity is only one of three possible underlying causes of malnutrition – the others being poor childcare and a poor public health environment and access to healthcare. Therefore, decision-makers wanting to use both HEA and nutrition data may want to ask the following questions:
- What can HEA tell us about dietary quality?
- What can HEA tell us about the causes of malnutrition?
- What can HEA tell us about the risk of malnutrition in the future?

Dietary quality
HEA is best suited to assessing whether access to macronutrients is sufficient. When discussing access to food, HEA typically focuses on energy (kcals), but it is relatively easy to add further analysis of access to protein and fat, as information on the sources of those macronutrients is collected as a matter of course. While an analysis of types of food accessed in HEA gives some broad indication of differences in dietary diversity between wealth groups, access to micronutrients is more difficult to assess using HEA. Sufficient quantities of many vitamins and minerals are provided in relatively small quantities of certain foodstuffs, and HEA's quantification is usually not precise enough to capture this reliably. HEA can, however, indicate whether certain types of food are present in the diet or not, which can prompt further investigation into the risks of specific micronutrient deficiencies.

Causes of malnutrition
HEA assessments can tell us whether or not elevated levels of malnutrition in a population are caused by food insecurity. Where food access falls significantly below 100% of minimum calorie requirements, malnutrition will occur. Linking HEA and nutrition survey data more closely requires ensuring (1) that indicators of wealth are somehow included in a nutrition survey, so that the wealth group into which households fall can be determined, and (2) that the geographical coverage of both the HEA and nutrition survey is the same, or that the sampling for the nutrition survey has been designed in a way that enables analysis by livelihood zone to be done. While HEA cannot tell us if malnutrition is caused by poor health or caring practices, it can very usefully tell us whether poverty is hindering access to healthcare or to soap and other items for good hygiene, and it can tell us if a balanced diet is unaffordable or if infant care is being disrupted by the need for mothers to take on heavy workloads.

Future risks of malnutrition

Because HEA is a predictive tool, we can indicate whether there is likely to be food insecurity in the future that could lead to malnutrition. While the diversity of factors that goes into determining nutritional outcomes makes precise prediction of malnutrition rates impossible, statements about future risks can be made on the basis of HEA outcomes by considering three issues:

- the time it may take for coping strategies – including harmful ones that may be used before food consumption is significantly reduced – to be exhausted
- the likely size of the deficit – while a 10% deficit at a point in time may not cause malnutrition, a 50% deficit is certainly going to cause problems
- the seasonality and timing of the deficit – a 17% deficit spread evenly throughout the year sounds bad, but not awful; but if that annual deficit is concentrated in just two months of the year, it translates into a very serious deficit of 100% for those two months.

Monitoring HEA predictions using nutritional status data is made more difficult, however, because nutritional status is generally considered a relatively late indicator, since unless there is displacement of a population or other sudden cutting-off of access to food, it usually takes some weeks or even months for the effect of a shock to show itself in changes in nutritional status. With slow-onset disasters such as drought, the main diminution of access to food may come quite late in the process, and the nutritional effects some weeks after that, so that changes in nutritional status would be a particularly late indicator for monitoring.

In addition, it can be difficult to interpret malnutrition rates in a 'bad year' in the absence of 'normal situation' survey evidence referring to the same geographical area in the same season. Nutritional surveillance over any wide area – meaning the measurement of a sample within the population at regular intervals – is expensive and extremely rare, but it is the data from such a system that provides the most credible baseline for interpreting rates of malnutrition in a bad year. Nutrition surveys are more typically undertaken in response to crisis, and interpreting data in relation to such one-off, geographically and seasonally specific surveys can be very difficult.

However, the Malawi Integrated Nutrition and Food Security Surveillance System (run by the Ministry of Health/Action Against Hunger) is a good example of a system that relates nutritional outcomes to initial HEA predictions, in this case made by the Malawi VAC, thus (indirectly) monitoring the effectiveness of response programmes.[31]

HEA and market analysis

All populations to a greater or lesser extent rely on markets, either to purchase goods and services, or to earn an income. Access to markets and the ways that those markets function have a substantial effect on the household economy. Figure 24 summarises how an understanding of markets is relevant at different stages of HEA analysis.

Market analysis in HEA is based on information on patterns of trade and market functioning from key informants such as traders, district officials and village representatives, combined with secondary information such as historical price data. The most important markets in HEA tend to be those for staple foods, livestock and, to a lesser extent, casual labour. Other markets such as those for cash crops or minerals may also need to be considered.

Analysis of this information focuses on understanding:
- the extent to which different wealth groups depend on particular markets and are exposed to changes within them, such as an increase in grain prices, a fall in cash crop prices or wage rates, or a decline in the quantity of grain available for purchase
- the factors that need to be monitored in relation to possible market shocks, such as the availability of grain in markets within the livelihood zone; the supply of grain or the demand for labour in linked markets outside the livelihood zone; governmental regulation of markets; or the functioning of transport infrastructure
- how markets are affected by or react to different hazards – for example, what impact does a drought have on grain prices and the quantities available for sale? – and how this translates into impacts on the household economy.

Many HEA assessments have shown how changes in market conditions can translate into effects on livelihoods at the household level. In Binga, Zimbabwe, an HEA analysis in 2001 indicated how a relatively small drop in crop production would translate into a serious impact on the ability of poor casual labourers to get by, because an increase in competition for a limited amount of work would drive down wage rates. HEA analysis can also highlight

6 LOOKING FORWARD AND OUTWARD: LINKS TO OTHER APPROACHES AND ISSUES

Figure 24: How market analysis fits into the HEA framework

	HEA baseline			HEA outcome analysis			
	Step 1: Livelihood zoning	Step 2: Wealth breakdown	Step 3: Livelihoods strategies	Step 4: Problem specification	Step 5: Coping capacity/ Response strategies	Step 6: Scenario outcome	Response analysis
WHY you need to know it	Which areas have access to which markets is one of two main determinants of livelihood zone boundaries	Who is able to profit from their interaction with the market and who is not is a major determinant in the wealth breakdown	People either produce their food or they use the market to get it. The poorer the household, the more the market plays a role in obtaining food	Any shock – even a production shock – has market effects. And those market effects in turn have household consequences	People use the market to cope with shocks. They try to sell more food stocks, more livestock, more labour, etc. And they try to buy more food	Projections of food or income deficits will rest on assumptions about what will happen to a whole range of prices	The most appropriate response to a food or livelihood crisis will often involve using the market. Markets help channel goods in an efficient manner
WHAT you need to know	We need to know where people sell their wares (livestock, labour, crops, etc) both within the country and across the border	We need to understand the connections between households in the community, and how households translate – through market interactions – their assets into different levels of wealth	We need to understand just how much food and how much cash income different wealth groups obtain through market mechanisms	We need to be able to understand what has happened, and what will happen to the prices of the things people sell and buy as this will affect their purchasing power	We need to understand both the opportunities the market presents as well as its limits as a coping response	We need to be able to make the best predictions about prices And we need to be able to monitor these prices against the thresholds set in the scenarios	We need to know: 1. Whether prices will exceed the purchasing power of the people in crisis; 2. Whether the right commodities will be able to reach the markets where the people in crisis live
HOW you get it	Market mapping and Livelihood Zoning Format – Markets section	Baseline Assessment Interview Form 3 – Wealth breakdown section	Baseline Assessment Interview Form 2, Interview Form 4	Historical price trend data, Baseline Assessment Interview Form 2, Interview Form 1 – Hazards and timelines section	Analysis of labour and livestock markets (the limits of demand) Baseline Assessment Interview Form 3 – Bad year section	Historical price trend data, Baseline Assessment Interview Form 2	Market integration studies, Historical price trend analysis

111

questions on particular markets on which further research could be beneficial, or areas where, for example, the pattern of demand evident in an HEA inquiry seems not to accord with the pattern of supply. For example, the overwhelming reliance of poor households on local casual employment, or *ganyu*, in Malawi, in both 'normal' and bad years has seemed out of all proportion to the possible demand for such labour among better-off households. A better understanding of this particular labour market and of its underlying dynamics would contribute a great deal to an understanding of poor people's vulnerability to drought.

The use of more specialised market analysis in conjunction with HEA assessments can provide additional insight into the range of interventions that might be appropriate in tackling longer-term problems. For example, an HEA study carried out in north-east Turkana in Kenya in 2006 was undertaken in tandem with a market analysis[32] which looked in greater depth at the markets (in grain and livestock particularly) on which households depend. This analysis was particularly important, as the poor functioning of the markets was a key constraint to any attempts at strengthening livelihoods in the area. Volumes traded were low and transaction costs were high, and improving conditions for traders was identified as a vital component of

> The use of more specialised market analysis alongside HEA assessments can be useful in filling information gaps and in identifying appropriate interventions.

any package to revitalise the area's economy. Possible measures included facilitating better coordination among individual traders to reduce transaction costs, support to the infrastructure, including the improvement of roads and communications such as mobile phone networks, and giving traders more options on where to buy and sell.

Similarly, an HEA assessment of informal mining communities in Zimbabwe indicated that miners were earning only Z$7,000 per ton of chrome mined, while the international mining company that was at the end of the market chain was buying that chrome at Z$70,000 per ton. The use of supply chain analysis to explain the difference in the two figures could usefully have fed into further inquiry into appropriate interventions for supporting the miners' livelihoods in the long term.

Detailed, formal market studies and analyses such as those carried out by WFP for its Strengthening Emergency Needs Assessment Capacity (SENAC) project, and work by FEWS-NET on informal cross-border trade in southern Africa, can also provide useful information for HEA analysis.

HEA and political economy analysis

Political economy analysis is based on the idea that patterns of asset ownership and of access to food and income among different wealth groups are very much related to who has power and how it is exercised. In these terms, an analysis of power at different levels is necessary to explain the causes of food insecurity. Political economy analysis has been described as "focusing on the distribution of power and wealth between different groups and individuals, and on the processes that create, sustain and transform these relationships over time".[33]

Power can affect food security at different levels. Within the household, for example, gender roles determine who does what work, whether women have control over the use of assets and income, and whether women can inherit land and other assets. At a higher level, power relations can also be the cause of competition for access to land or grazing rights, which can lead to conflict, or of competition for political power, which can lead to marginalisation and discrimination. All of these influence the livelihood strategies that different people can pursue.

An understanding of political economy can, therefore, contribute to food security analysis and programming in three ways. First, it can provide a deeper understanding of the social and political causes of poverty and food insecurity which can sometimes – if rarely – be addressed by humanitarian agencies. Second, it can help predict the problems that may arise as a result of conflict between different groups. Third, it can help ensure sensitivity to power relationships and potential for conflict in the programming of interventions.

Although a limited investigation into power relations can be incorporated within an HEA assessment, it can be more useful for a complementary political economy analysis to be carried out using checklists and tools specifically developed for that purpose. These tend to use the same field methods (key informants and semi-structured interviews) as those used within HEA and they include the 'Social Relations Framework', the 'Local Capacities for Peace

Framework', and conflict analysis tools such as the UK Department for International Development's (DFID's) 'Conducting Conflict Assessments: Guidance Notes'. This sort of analysis will complement standard HEA results well. HEA assessments indicate who is food insecure, when, and to what extent, and can indicate aspects of livelihoods that are weakest, while a greater understanding of power will provide insight into the causes of food insecurity. It can also help determine which livelihood support options are most likely to be successful and what social and political issues may need to be addressed to tackle the root causes of poverty.

> Political economy analysis can provide a deeper understanding of the social and political causes of poverty and can therefore complement HEA inquiries well.

6.3 How HEA can contribute to particular issues

Using HEA to distinguish between chronic and transitory food insecurity

Food security questions go beyond drought and 'bad years' to more permanent circumstances for considerable numbers of people in southern Africa. The chronically food insecure are those who either consistently fail, year on year, to meet their full energy requirements, or those who live so 'close to the edge' that any small shock can tip them into crisis. It is important for policy-makers to differentiate between the chronically food insecure and those with a temporary inability to access sufficient food as a result of a shock, since the distinction has implications for response: a short-term relief intervention that will help fill the deficit of the transitorily food insecure will not be an appropriate measure for addressing the fundamentally different problems of the chronically food insecure.

The chronically food insecure are commonly those existing on the edge of a given economic mode of life, and in this sense 'marginal'. They tend to lack productive assets, whether in land, livestock or labour. Many elderly-headed households, for example, lack the strength to work, and those who lack kinship links or other means of community support can find themselves unable to earn

6 LOOKING FORWARD AND OUTWARD: LINKS TO OTHER APPROACHES AND ISSUES

a living. Others may be able-bodied but, as in the case of youths in some communities, lack access to other assets such as land or skills. Others again – such as those widowed women whose inheritance rights are not respected – may have had their assets taken away or be otherwise unable to use them. All these groups may be chronically food insecure, but the appropriate response to each situation varies. The first group may be best supported through old age pensions or some other form of social protection; the second needs support that will enable them to become productive and 'graduate' from poverty; while the third group may need policy measures or legal support to maintain their entitlements.

> **Identifying how the chronically food insecure can be supported involves looking at the particular constraints of different groups within this category.**

HEA can be used as a tool both to distinguish the chronically food insecure from those who are facing transitory food insecurity, and as a means of understanding the characteristics of the chronically poor and possible means of supporting them. HEA tries to understand typical livelihoods patterns, vulnerabilities and hazards, and differences between good, bad and average years. With this information we can see which groups are struggling even in the absence of external shocks. Those groups who are unable to meet their minimum food energy needs even in an average year can be considered chronically food insecure. Those who can normally manage but as a result of a hazard are unable to meet their food needs at a particular point in time can be considered transitorily food insecure.

Another question for policy-makers is the extent to which the transitorily food insecure will be able to recover: have they been pushed over the edge? By reviewing their assets and the sustainability of their livelihood strategies (are they drawing down on a limited supply of assets? Or are they actually accumulating capital holdings of some kind?), we can model further in advance and see whether people risk getting caught in a poverty trap that will eventually lead to chronic food insecurity.

Because the chronically food insecure can be a relatively heterogeneous group, an investigation into their circumstances using HEA may need to disaggregate the poorer wealth groups further to be of practical use. Ways in which this can be done are outlined in 'Disaggregated variants of HEA' in section 4.3.

Using HEA to measure levels of poverty

HEA can be used to measure and compare levels of poverty within and across geographic areas. Ultimately, wealth is a measure of how much people can obtain with what they have available. HEA helps get at this through converting all sources of food and income to a common currency – the ratio between calories required for the household, in annual terms, and those provided by the source of food or income. So, for instance, it is possible to express different ways of obtaining food (production vs purchase) and different types of crops (cassava vs maize) in the same terms (% of annual food needs met), which allows you to compare the relative importance (in food terms) of these different sources.

This way of measuring poverty has distinct advantages over two other frequently employed methods: that of comparing against a minimum income threshold, and consumption surveys. Income in rural areas is often hidden, with local labour, gifts and petty trade often falling through the gaps. Consumption surveys, on the other hand, are a reflection of choice as much as access, and say little about people's assets and income sources. HEA captures the full range of reported income and food options, making it possible to see clear differences in real wealth between households.

There are two ways that HEA typically expresses this measurement. It can do so firstly in terms of 'food income', and secondly in terms of 'maximum access'. **Food income** simply means the total amount of food produced, purchased or received by the household in a typical year. Figure 25 provides an example of how this kind of analysis provides an interesting basic comparison of poor household wealth across very different country contexts.

While this is the simplest way to express the measurement, and can be useful in certain contexts, it leaves out most income as well as assets such as livestock, which together usually comprise a substantial proportion of household wealth. **Maximum access** is, therefore, a more inclusive way of measuring poverty, because it takes account of all food produced, all income potentially earned, and all convertible assets. In other words, if all of a household's potential food

6 LOOKING FORWARD AND OUTWARD: LINKS TO OTHER APPROACHES AND ISSUES

Figure 25: Comparing poverty using 'food income'

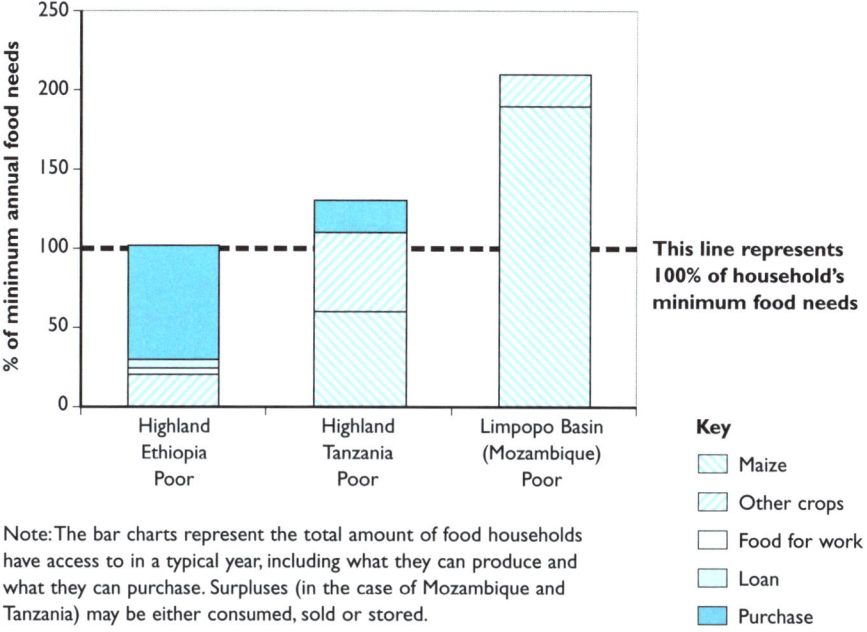

Note: The bar charts represent the total amount of food households have access to in a typical year, including what they can produce and what they can purchase. Surpluses (in the case of Mozambique and Tanzania) may be either consumed, sold or stored.

production, income earnings and productive assets could be converted into food, maximum access shows how much of a year's food requirements this would cover for a household.

Figure 26 (overleaf), for instance, shows that poor households in the Eastern Livelihood Zone in Tanzania could potentially cover around 150% of their annual food needs if they maximised all of their livelihood strategies. We know that households do not maximise their access to food in most years, choosing instead to put assets in reserve for other purposes. Maximum access is, therefore, not meant to be an illustration of what people *actually* do, but rather a measurement of what they would be able to obtain if they had to. In that sense, it provides a useful tool for comparing household economic potential or wealth.

• THE HOUSEHOLD ECONOMY APPROACH

Figure 26: Comparing poverty using 'maximum access'

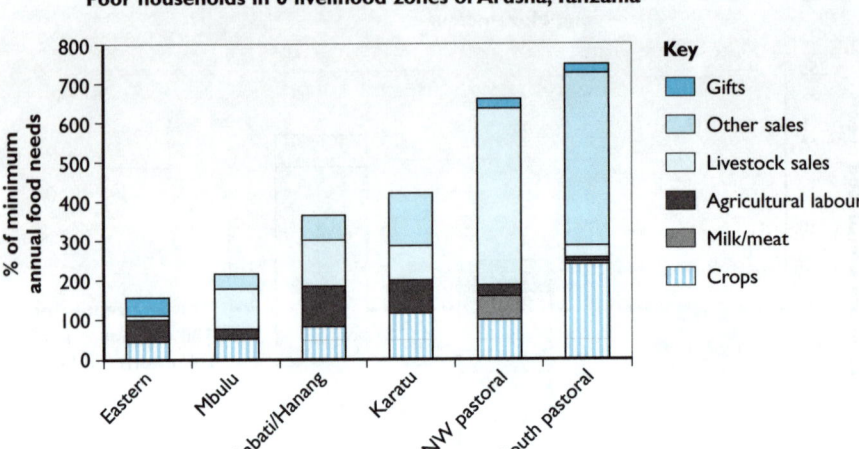

Note: The bar graphs represent 'maximum access', or the total amount of food and income (converted into kilo-calorie equivalents) available to households based on reference year production and price data. In other words, the bars show just how much of the household's annual calorie requirements could be covered if it converted all of its assets (food production, income generation, productive capital, etc) into food.

Source: Based on analysis conducted by Tanya Boudreau using data gathered during an assessment organised by Save the Children, the Government of Tanzania and WFP

Using HEA to understand and address the needs of specific groups: the examples of children and HIV/AIDS-affected families

A 'classic' HEA assessment provides household economy information by wealth group within each livelihood zone. However, certain users may need information on specific sub-sections of the population other than wealth groups. These may be demographic groups such as children, the elderly or women,[34] or groups defined in social, cultural or economic terms such as those affected by HIV and AIDS, specific ethnic minorities, or people doing a specific livelihoods activity (such as sex workers). When considering such groups, decision-makers are typically interested in:
• What differentiates them from other groups in terms of their livelihood activities and their food security or overall wealth?

- What particular needs do they have and/or what specific interventions would be most suited to their circumstances?

The HEA framework can be used, with minor adaptations, to field methods to look into these questions. To illustrate, we can consider two typical areas of research: the situation of HIV/AIDS-affected households, and the situation of children within families.

Using HEA to understand the needs of HIV/AIDS-affected households

In recent years, the links between HIV and AIDS, food security and livelihoods have been the subject of much research and many direct interventions. The impact of HIV and AIDS on livelihoods are multiple and diverse: it can reduce the ability of sick household members to work; increase the demands on remaining household members' time to care for the ill; increase the burden of healthcare costs; and lead to problems with the inheritance by the bereaved of land and other assets. The ways in which different aspects of the household economy can be affected by HIV and AIDS is illustrated in Figure 27 (overleaf).

The HEA framework can be used to examine the situation of HIV/AIDS-affected households and to illustrate the effects of HIV and AIDS. In this case, we would take our baseline as being the period before the effects of HIV and AIDS were felt, and look at assets, food, income and expenditure as usual. HIV and AIDS would then be treated as a shock, or as a collection of shocks, with those affected providing information both on how they have been affected and how they have responded. For example, the problem specification may show that the loss of labour as a result of illness caused a 100% loss of casual labour income if the ill household member was the only one working, or a 300% increase in the cost of healthcare, etc. The response may be, for example, an increase in the number of livestock sold as a coping mechanism, or in an increase in work by other members of the household to compensate for the loss of labour of the ill member.

The added value of HEA in this case is that it gives a holistic view of the impacts of HIV and AIDS, rather than focusing on, for example, the impacts on agricultural production alone. It enables us to see how the household adapts to the illness, recognising that while the overall impact will almost invariably be negative, households will try to re-allocate their labour and other assets to minimise those negative impacts.

Figure 27: HIV and AIDS and the household economy

Sources of food

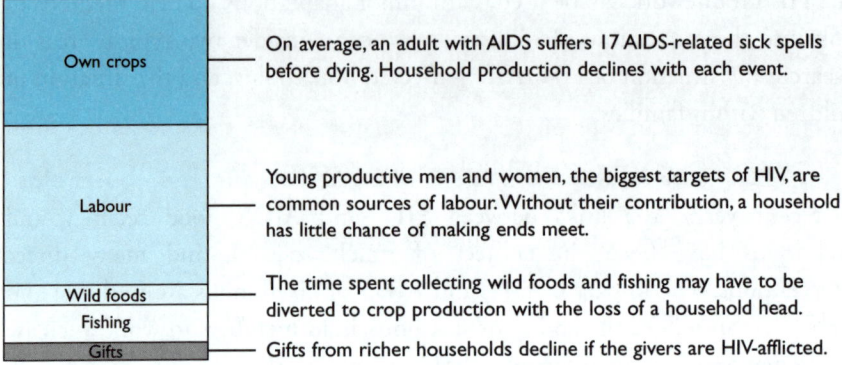

On average, an adult with AIDS suffers 17 AIDS-related sick spells before dying. Household production declines with each event.

Young productive men and women, the biggest targets of HIV, are common sources of labour. Without their contribution, a household has little chance of making ends meet.

The time spent collecting wild foods and fishing may have to be diverted to crop production with the loss of a household head.

Gifts from richer households decline if the givers are HIV-afflicted.

Sources of cash

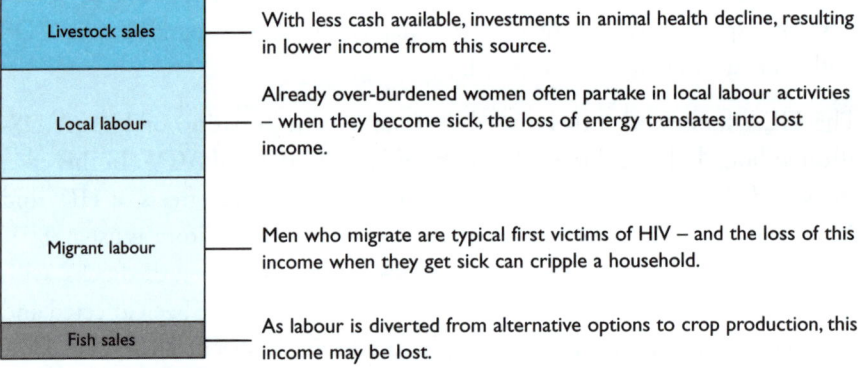

With less cash available, investments in animal health decline, resulting in lower income from this source.

Already over-burdened women often partake in local labour activities – when they become sick, the loss of energy translates into lost income.

Men who migrate are typical first victims of HIV – and the loss of this income when they get sick can cripple a household.

As labour is diverted from alternative options to crop production, this income may be lost.

Expenditure patterns

Discretionary expenditure quickly disappears as health costs rise, leaving families unable to cope with unexpected outlays or increased food purchases in a bad year.

One in four children in sub-Saharan Africa has lost at least one parent to AIDS. For families who foster orphaned children, relative expenditure on food increases, putting these households closer to the edge and less able to recover from cyclical droughts or other shocks.

Expenditure on basic goods, such as salt and soap, are compromised by increased expenditures on food and health.

Rising health expenditure and funeral costs force households to choose between essentials, like food and school.

In terms of the methods needed for collecting this information, some adaptation of the purposive sampling normally used for HEA assessments is required, in that it is necessary to define quite clearly the type of people who will be interviewed in order to get the clearest results. For example, the broad category of 'HIV/AIDS-affected' can include families with someone who is chronically ill, families who have recently lost an income-earner, or families who have taken in an orphaned child. The nature of the 'shock' resulting from HIV and AIDS may differ significantly in each case, and so care should be taken not to over-aggregate information by placing all HIV/AIDS-affected families in a single category. Similarly, disaggregating by wealth remains necessary, as the impact of HIV and AIDS on a family that was initially better off could vary substantially from the impact on a poor family, especially in the short term. Because of the sensitivity of the issue of HIV and AIDS in some cases, it may be more effective to interview people on an individual basis rather than in focus groups.

Once information on HIV/AIDS-affected families has been collected, then their status can be compared with those unaffected. But to do so effectively, it is again vital to ensure that you are comparing the affected and unaffected within the same wealth group. Comparing, for example an affected family from a better-off background with an unaffected family from a poor background would produce confusing results. This type of comparison is also important as a means of trying to separate out the effects of other shocks from the shock of HIV and AIDS. For example, if there has also been a drought between the baseline period and the current period, then it is useful to compare the change over time between affected and unaffected households to try to determine how much of the change for the affected households is caused by HIV and AIDS and how much by drought.

Using HEA to understand the needs of children

Considering the situation of children within HEA involves incorporating the same kind of sensitivity that can be given to power or conflict or gender issues. It does not require changes to the framework or major changes to field methods.

Within most recent HEA assessments by Save the Children, an effort has been made to consider (1) how children contribute to the livelihood of their family and (2) how their family's livelihood affects not only children's access to food, but other aspects of their welfare, such as access to education and healthcare, or the risk of abuse or exploitation.

In the first case, the work goes beyond classic HEA analysis by looking more systematically at who does what within the household. This, equally, could be applied to considering the roles of women or the elderly. In assessments to date, the information for children has been gathered by talking directly to boys and girls of different ages, in addition to including it in discussions with parents. The direct discussions with children have on occasion been found to reveal activities that children engage in of which parents are largely unaware, such as small-scale hunting and the selling of birds and small animals in Zimbabwe, or activities that parents are reluctant to discuss, such as sending children from poor families to do paid domestic work for better-off families in Ethiopia.

By getting a clearer sense of children's roles, the impact on children of hazards can also be understood more thoroughly and the implications highlighted for decision-makers. For example, is there a risk that increased casual labouring will mean increased child labour? Might there be an increase in dangerous forms of labour undertaken by children, such as mining? Might girls be exposed to greater risk of sexual exploitation if coping strategies include transactional sex or sending girls away for domestic work? This sort of analysis is vital both for strengthening the case for fast and adequate response to emerging livelihoods problems, and for encouraging responses that go beyond traditional food-focused activities.

7 Limits and criticisms of HEA

The application of HEA in the field of early warning and emergency needs assessment has been tested and developed over more than a decade in a range of conditions and different contexts. Over the same period, the approach has been adapted and used for other purposes, such as the identification and design of poverty reduction and social protection strategies. This history and range of experience has entailed methodological adaptations and the development of new tools, and some of the criticisms levelled at HEA in its early days no longer apply. For example, HEA was originally criticised for focusing too much on emergency response and food aid requirements, and for not being applicable in urban contexts or situations of conflict. Its wider application as described in Chapter 2, 'How has HEA been used?', has shown that it adapts well to different contexts and purposes.

Learning from experience should include continued attention to criticism. The only caveat is that the criticism should be about things HEA can reasonably be expected to do. There are, of course, many aspects of project planning and implementation for which HEA does not provide information, and these are listed in Table 12 overleaf.

It is also worth bearing in mind that the central subject that HEA does tackle – the assessment of livelihoods under pressure – is by no means simple. The challenge for HEA has been to construct a practical field approach for identifying the threshold between poverty and livelihood failure – or between poverty and livelihood security – and to do so in a quantified way. Such differences are often delicate and difficult to discern, and no one with experience of the rigours of field work wishes to make the task more difficult than it has to be. Adaptations to the approach will continue to be made; however, such adaptations must always consider the

> **The assessment of poor people's livelihoods in relation to thresholds that are delicate and difficult to discern will never be easy.**

THE HOUSEHOLD ECONOMY APPROACH

Table 12: What HEA does not provide

- macroeconomic analysis
- direct political and social analysis
- analysis of food 'utilisation' in the sense of the absorption of nutrients by the body; or analysis of dietary quality and micronutrient deficiencies
- an analysis of the operational feasibility of implementing particular projects
- information on the delivery infrastructure and logistics
- an analysis of market infrastructure/viability
- detailed information on targeting such as distribution lists[35]
- an analysis of the political considerations in deciding on one type of intervention over another
- a wider environmental or anthropological analysis of project impact: can the environment support more livestock? Might the project exacerbate intra- or inter-community relations? How might it affect patterns of reciprocity between the poor and the better off?
- analysis of the political context of an humanitarian crisis.

Note: Should these things be needed by decision-makers and should the necessary skills and resources be available, they could be done in conjunction with an HEA assessment.

---

trade-offs between the detail and relevance of the information sought and the time and money required for field work and analysis.

Criticisms made of HEA include the following:

HEA requires high calibre staff and a lot of training

Conducting an HEA investigation in the field *is* a technically demanding task. This is not a questionnaire system, with field assistants or enumerators filling in forms and with the entire data analysis carried out by someone else later. A successful 'household economist' has to be a clear analyst as well as a rigorous field worker. HEA field staff must fully grasp not only the key information requirements but the concepts which have generated them: as far as possible the information has to make sense as it is recorded in the field, and where it does not, that must prompt further questions.

HEA field work does not require people with higher degrees – or any degrees at all. But it does ask a lot from field workers and this means that more time is required for staff training than for a typical sample survey. An apt person will need about one week's 'desk' training on the concepts and procedures, but the rest of the standard training tends to be 'on the job', doing field interviews; and this should be under the supervision of an experienced team leader. As with most technical skills, practice counts heavily. While these demands are in one sense a drawback, they also have their benefits. These include capacity-building: staff develop a better understanding of the concepts of livelihoods and food security in general, and of the areas and populations under investigation in particular. There is also a much greater sense among staff of shared ownership of the analysis and, therefore, of the output. In this way, an HEA assessment is not only an exercise in obtaining information, but a process of building the confidence and capacity of staff to construct an account of livelihoods for themselves. For those staff who are also involved in designing and implementing interventions, these skills can enhance their work considerably.

> HEA field work is technically demanding and requires staff to be well trained. But this has benefits in terms of capacity-building and in terms of a greater sense of shared ownership among staff of the analysis.

Investigators in any kind of survey have to understand the basics of the subject they are inquiring into, otherwise the questions are likely to be posed badly. They also have to understand how to do the minimum of basic cross-checking and they have to be sufficiently committed to the exercise to not simply sit under a tree and fill in the interview formats themselves. The pertinent point is not that HEA methods themselves require high-quality and trained staff, but that high-calibre staff are needed by any method that seeks to provide valid and convincing data on livelihoods.

HEA is expensive

This criticism often attaches to the foregoing. Yet unlike sample surveys involving large numbers of field enumerators, for coverage of the same population HEA typically involves two to four teams of around four people; the field methods of HEA are, after all, those of rapid appraisal. But the expense referred to is usually that of international consultants – for training, field work planning, and field team leadership or supervision; for helping with the analysis and write-up; and for leading the use of the data for situation-monitoring or other purposes. There is no question that international consultants are expensive compared with local consultants or the time of government professionals. This, of course, is not a problem exclusive to HEA: many surveys of other types involve the use of international staff. However, it is an issue that needs to be confronted.

One-off HEA exercises are inevitably more expensive if local staff are not capable of running them. The capacity-building referred to in relation to the first criticism above comes strongly into focus here. HEA has become institutionalised in a number of places, including Malawi, Somalia and Ethiopia, and national staff increasingly run the show. HEA is at its best and least expensive when it involves continuity and 'nationalisation', so that local staff run the training and the other steps listed above, while international consultants may be called in only for quite specific and short tasks. In that case, HEA can actually be cheaper in terms of personnel/time than many other survey procedures.

Another criticism is that HEA baselines are expensive to develop, in terms of personnel time and logistics. Again, this is true of many surveys. But a baseline is almost by definition something that is referred to for a long time afterwards. For instance, the baseline developed by the Malawi VAC in 2002/03 has been used for national assessments in all the subsequent years; so one has to see the investment in the HEA baseline work in terms of its utility over time. It is usually thought that baseline information will be valid for at least five years unless a major event changes the fundamental livelihoods picture (see 'Use of baselines', in section 2.4). Even then, the cost of updating a baseline is likely to be considerably less than that of developing it in the first instance.

> The cost of developing an HEA baseline should be seen in terms of its utility over time, since the same baseline data can normally be used over several years.

But in the end there is no getting away from the fact that good-quality information has a cost. HEA allows opportunities for short cuts in information-collection and is remarkably flexible and adaptable. But there is a 'bottom line': there is no point in attempting an HEA exercise without the minimum resources to provide a reliable result. And experience has shown time and again that in the long run, the cost of decisions made on the basis of poor information can be very high, in terms of missed opportunities to limit suffering as well as material wastage.

HEA assessments take too long

The time taken to do an HEA assessment is to a great extent determined by the resources available and the purpose for which the baseline information will be used. An indication of the time necessary for different types of assessment is given in section 4.4. Experience has shown that, despite the HEA requirement to cross-check and discuss information as it is being collected in the field, the time taken for both the field work and the analysis is actually short compared with most sample surveys that collect similar information, and for which results are rarely available until at least a month (and often much longer) after the completion of the field work.

HEA lacks statistical rigour

This criticism is usually based on the notion that the only 'real' information is that based on statistically based sample surveys. However, statistical approaches are not the only form of 'rigour'. Statisticians will be the first to point out that random-based or probability statistical sampling may guarantee an equal chance for people to be represented in a given area, but in no way guarantees the accuracy of reported data. Whether data is collected by means of statistically sampled household interviews or through interviews of carefully identified and compared focus groups, what is important is how well it is done – and what means there are to promote accuracy. This is discussed in Chapter 5, 'Is HEA reliable?'.

> Random or other statistical sampling may guarantee an equal chance for people to be represented in a given area, but it does not guarantee the accuracy of their response to questions.

HEA is methodologically rigid

The idea of a methodology does imply a certain integrity of framework and procedures that distinguish it clearly from others. If that is defined as rigidity, then any methodology worth its salt must be 'rigid'. For HEA, a change away from the household as the primary reference point, or from the analysis of food and cash sources and expenditure as primary procedures, would be a fundamental challenge to the methodology as such. This does not mean that a methodology cannot be adapted for different purposes; nor does it mean that a methodology should be blind to possible improvements that emanate from other methods or approaches. But unless the core of the methodology is unsound, an 'improvement' cannot be something that fundamentally alters the framework and procedures, even in the name of collegiality or 'harmonisation'. Similarly, this does not mean that HEA as a methodology should not expect – and indeed endeavour – to sit usefully beside other methodologies, such as nutritional survey or social

> That methodologies can inform and complement each other does not mean that they can or should be somehow merged, unless the advantages and feasibility of merging them are clear.

inquiry – usefully in the sense that each tries to inform the other. But again, this does not mean that methodologies can or should be somehow merged, unless a detailed and practical case is made for both the feasibility and the advantage of merging them.

At another level, the criticism of rigidity has sometimes referred to HEA's strong association with one approach to collecting field information: rapid appraisal. While this is not so much a rigid adherence to one method as a reflection of its successful application over many years, it is important to recognise that HEA is a framework that can use a broad range of tools for information collection, including household sample surveys, depending on the purpose of the inquiry.

HEA is food-oriented and does not consider non-food issues such as water, health and education

Like any other practical methodology, HEA does not seek to be 'all things to all men' or claim coverage of, and skills in, areas attended to by other specialists. But because the analysis of livelihoods is of considerable relevance to a number of such areas, there may sometimes be an expectation that HEA include direct study of them. Clearly, where an assessment seeks to investigate the economic constraints to access to certain services, or, say, the impact of long-term illness on households' ability to survive, HEA information collection and analysis are constructed around these requirements.[36] Such inquiries can also provide a useful entry point for looking at non-economic barriers to healthcare and education. But these are HEA investigations with a focus on a particular sector. Information systems that seek to tackle a question as difficult as determining which groups will fall below a certain livelihood threshold in the future should not be expected, whatever the methodology, to include a meaningful study of other sectors.

This criticism can also relate to the practicalities of information collection. Detailed field work organised to represent large rural areas can be sufficiently rare that colleagues in other sectors may want to add some elements of inquiry – for example, into villagers' use or views of health or education facilities – which may not be relevant to the focal question of the HEA analysis. Often, colleagues may not realise just how much effort is involved in obtaining the basic HEA field data in the time usually available, and how much of a burden additional questions may present. Constructive working together to look at how analyses of different issues complement each other is, needless to say, always welcome.

HEA is not useful in complex emergencies

Experience demonstrates that this is not the case: HEA has been used in several complex emergencies, ranging from Burundi to Somalia to Kosovo. What is true is that HEA is useful for looking at the economic aspects of such emergencies, such as household coping in terms of food and cash. It does not aim to provide an analysis of the wider social and political determinants of the crisis, although these are naturally taken into account when looking at economic coping. The links between HEA and political economy analysis are discussed in section 6.2.

HEA does not adequately analyse non-economic root causes of poverty

That is true: HEA is not designed to do this, and does not claim to. HEA is an economic analysis, and would need to be combined with additional tools to analyse non-economic factors in depth. However, HEA might be considered as one of many approaches or specialisms that have something indirect but important to contribute to such analysis of non-economic factors. The holistic description of livelihoods strategies and assets offers a remarkably acute view of poverty – for instance, of the resource constraints faced by poor people, and how they try to maximise what they

> HEA describes in detail wealth divisions that are often all but invisible to outsiders, but which reflect among other things differential political and social power and influence.

can do with what they have. It describes in detail wealth divisions that are often all but invisible to outsiders, but which reflect among other things differential political and social power and influence. This interface between the economic and the non-economic enables HEA to help identify in broad terms the non-economic root causes of poverty, whether these be political marginalisation and insecurity, as in the Turkana region in Kenya (see section 3.5), or inequitable land distribution, as in the Thar Desert in Pakistan (section 3.4). Further analysis of such structural determinants of poverty is the province of other specialists.

HEA does not link community-level and macro-level analysis

HEA connects directly with the wider political economy, from land law to the wider market system, in two respects. First, it is inevitably the context within which an HEA baseline is constructed, since it forms the operating environment that ultimately defines the local constraints and opportunities that people must negotiate to run their livelihoods. Second, as a result of this connection, macro-level changes in the economy, for example, through changes in market access, or the introduction of new pricing policies, or changes in levels of or access to state benefits, can be imposed on baseline HEA information to assess the impact on people's exchange entitlements at the household level.

> **HEA inevitably connects with the wider political economy, since this is the operating environment that defines people's constraints and opportunities.**

To this extent, HEA links to the macro level. However, HEA does not in itself include macro-level analysis either of the wider national economy or of the political and social changes that impinge on it. That is the job of other specialists, just as it is not usually the job or skill of these specialists to analyse the effects of such changes at the household level. But HEA practitioners should make a point of taking account of the analyses available at the wider level, and should seize upon any practical suggestion from other specialists as to how to do this better.

HEA does not offer the disaggregated information necessary for social protection design or targeting

While HEA analysis is usually conducted on wealth groups, for reasons described in section 2.4, the framework does not preclude the study of groups of households defined by demographic characteristics. Different sampling and analytical methods can be used to look at different groups, and this is discussed in section 4.3, while the use of HEA to understand the needs of specific groups, such as children or HIV-affected households, is discussed in section 6.3.

HEA is not a 'one size fits all' methodology; the methods by which HEA information is gathered and analysed continue to be adapted and developed for particular purposes. Most recently, this has been to help in the identification and design of social protection interventions, and a combination of different methods have been used in order to look at questions of interest for policy-makers (see section 4.3).

It is worth pointing out, however, that the wealth of detail offered by an HEA analysis that looks at four wealth groups already adds very great value to the design and targeting of social protection transfers (see section 3.5). HEA data can be used to compile cut-offs for livestock and land ownership, which can then be used to identify poor households requiring safety net support.[37] The characteristics of the 'very poor' or 'poor' wealth groups identified (by local communities) in an HEA assessment can be turned into targeting criteria, which can then be 'passed back' to community leaders or committees to identify individual households eligible for assistance.

However, it is important to note that targeting is rarely achieved by any kind of survey, except nutritional anthropometry aimed at screening children for special feeding programmes. Otherwise, targeting is either administrative – that is, beneficiaries are officially selected according to a given criterion, such as owning no livestock, female-headed, disabled – or it is community-based, performed by village committees according to given parameters, such as the poorest 25% of households. Whether the application of criteria identified in an HEA-type vulnerability assessment can be more accurate, timely and cost-effective than such community-based targeting – for which approaches to reduce the problems of nepotism and exclusion have been developed – is an open question.

HEA does not consider intra-household issues

This is broadly true. The HEA framework is based on the economic activities of households, not individuals, since the household is the smallest economic unit by which people manage and within which decisions related to acquiring food and cash, allocating labour and accessing basic goods and services are made. It is difficult to analyse individuals' access to food and income outside this context in any meaningful way. In HEA, we can ask about which household members are involved in different activities, but we often cannot precisely quantify the economic contributions of individual household members, nor their personal consumption of goods and services. However, the household is arguably the smallest unit at which it is effective to target support, at least in terms of programmes that aim to provide food or non-food economic support. Issues of intra-household sharing of resources, or childcare behaviour, or decisions about who should be sent to school, are for other programmes and other analyses.

> In HEA, while we can ask which household members are involved in different activities, we often cannot precisely quantify the economic contributions of individual members, nor their personal consumption of goods and services.

HEA does not take into account differences in livelihood within a livelihood zone

Sometimes, groups of people living in the same livelihood zone pursue quite different patterns of livelihood, not because of differences in wealth, but for cultural reasons or because of differences in ethnicity. For example, a lakeshore zone might have two different groups living side by side: cattle-keepers who do not fish and fisherfolk who keep a few cattle. If these differences in livelihood are not just reflections of differences in wealth, then two patterns of livelihood need to be defined. The fact that the groups pursuing these patterns of livelihood live in exactly the same geographical area does not really matter; the two groups are simply considered as separate livelihoods.

But should different ethnic groups living in the same livelihood zone be analysed as separate groups? The important point here is that the economic vulnerability of ethnic groups is still defined by their livelihood patterns; how they will respond to a particular shock depends on their ability to access the food, income and basic services they need. Of course, livelihoods are defined in part according to households' access to social and political networks; but what matters here is how such networks affect access to land, or employment, or gifts of food, rather than the social and political environment itself. This is an analysis that requires them to be grouped according to livelihood, rather than ethnicity.

> How an ethnic group will respond to a shock depends on their ability to access the food, income and services they need. Access to social and political networks, defined by their ethnicity, is just one determinant of this.

On a related note, it is true that certain ethnic groups are more likely to be exposed to particular hazards such as looting or cattle-raiding. But the critical task is to group people according to what is effectively their capacity to cope, rather than to the probability of a shock occurring.

HEA is based on a 'normal' year, which in reality does not exist

HEA practice does not seek to define a 'normal' year, but instead identifies a 'reference year' for which baseline information is then gathered. This enables monitoring data in subsequent years to be compared with that in the reference or baseline year. More on the reference year and how it is chosen can be found in section 4.1.

HEA analysis does not correspond with administrative boundaries

This is discussed in 'Livelihood zones and administrative divisions' in section 2.4.

8 What are the products of HEA and how can they be used?

As described in Chapter 3, HEA has been used over the past decade in a number of ways to inform decision-making, ranging from early warning of food security and emergency and post-emergency needs assessments through to poverty analysis, the identification of poverty reduction strategies and the determination of safety net levels.

Different uses and users clearly require different outputs, and HEA investigations have led to a range of products that attempt to respond to decision-makers' specific needs in each case. In addition, the steps involved in creating an HEA baseline have generated products that have themselves been found to have uses beyond HEA investigations. The products arising from both HEA baselines and outcome analysis are shown in Table 13 (opposite). This section gives a brief outline of some of these products.

8.1 Products from an outcome analysis

Decision-maker briefs

A decision-maker brief is a one- or two-page briefing paper designed to convey an important message to people with limited time. Its key features are that it is short, concise and delivers only necessary information. In contrast to academic papers, it starts with the conclusion and then provides the relevant supporting evidence.

FEWS NET Alerts are good examples of such briefing papers. When a food crisis begins to emerge, FEWS NET issues alerts to decision-makers that provide specific information on causes and effects of the developing crisis, incorporating HEA analysis where it is available. This helps decision-makers and planners prepare for and respond to these crises. Similarly, FEWS NET's Executive Overview Briefs provide executive decision-makers with an overview

8 WHAT ARE THE PRODUCTS OF HEA AND HOW CAN THEY BE USED?

Table 13: Products of HEA

Framework step	Products
Baseline	• livelihood zone map library • wealth breakdowns provide basis for population estimates (combined with livelihood zoning) used in needs estimates • wealth breakdowns can be used to develop targeting criteria for identifying poor households requiring, eg, safety net support • livelihood profiles • thematic reports on particular subjects • seasonal calendars • full baseline reports • poverty analysis
Outcome analysis	• annual projections (eg, for Consolidated Appeals Process) • decision-maker briefs • assessment reports • presentations • monitoring framework

of the food security situation in Africa, based on FEWS NET's regular monitoring and reporting. They help decision-makers prioritise areas where action is needed most urgently.[38]

Reviews of vulnerability assessment practice in southern Africa have highlighted the importance of communicating VAC assessment results in a more accessible way, through "executive format bulletins, highly graphical in format that present bottom line answers or clearly articulated scenarios for decision-makers".[39]

Thematic briefs and reports

Briefs on particular subjects and customised for specific audiences tend to be slightly longer. Good examples of this kind of product are the Limpopo Development Brief or the Limpopo Food Aid Brief, both of which drew on information obtained during a baseline assessment in Mozambique's Limpopo Basin in 2001. Unlike the baseline report which was written to provide a repository of information about households in the livelihood zone, the briefs were written to address the concerns of specific target audiences. Table 14 shows just how different the sets of conclusions were for different audiences.

Table 14: Limpopo Basin, Mozambique: Targeted conclusions from thematic briefs

Food Aid Brief Conclusions	Development Brief Conclusions
1. **Non-emergency food aid is not likely to be an appropriate resource.** Risk-minimising agricultural practices and fertile soils along the river guarantee sufficient food for households from their own crops every year. Significant involvement in mining employment in South Africa ensures access to cash even in years of lower crop production. 2. **Food for work may not be an appropriate distribution mechanism** because labour, not land, is the biggest constraint to production in this area. With at least two cropping seasons, labour crunch times occur throughout the year. 3. **Food aid after a flood should be carefully targeted.** Only the 20% of households living along the river basin should be targeted, and only while markets are being restored. Once food is available in markets, households should be able to purchase food with remittance money from South Africa.	1. Development planners need to take into account that **this is a high risk, high return area**. Efforts of planners to maximise returns without considering households' risk-minimising strategies may increase vulnerability to floods. 2. Sales of cassava and tomatoes are the most important sources of cash for households with more than half a hectare. **Improved marketing of these cash crops** would increase incomes for rural households. 3. Animal traction fills an important labour gap. Continued **efforts at restocking and improved animal health** are well-placed. 4. Cashew trees were once an important source of cash income. **Replanting and maintenance of this resource** could bring additional income.

Source: FEWS NET/FEG[40]

Other examples of thematic reports that present the results of a targeted HEA analysis are those commissioned by Save the Children in Singida, Tanzania. One outlined a number of possible social protection measures that HEA analysis had modelled, while the other looked at whether the poor were economically constrained in their access to healthcare.[41]

Annual projection reports

Where the HEA framework is integrated within an early warning monitoring system, projections of food access over the coming six to 12 months are presented in annual or seasonal projection reports. A good example of this is the food security monitoring report for Malawi,[42] produced in May 2004 by the Malawi VAC using data from the monitoring system described in section 3.1. It provided:

- a national overview of projected food security in 2004, giving a national estimate of the missing food entitlement
- details of the expected conditions in each affected livelihood zone
- an appendix detailing the missing food entitlements and income requirements for each zone.

Assessment reports

Reports indicating how access to food and cash will be affected by one or more future hazards, or how an intervention might improve access to food and cash, are also products of one-off assessments commissioned by NGOs.

8.2 Products from an HEA baseline

Livelihood zone map

A livelihood zone map provides a division of the country into reasonably homogeneous zones defined according to patterns of livelihood. It is, thus, a means of dividing the population into groups for a range of analyses, and can provide a livelihoods basis for various types of survey or assessment, including emergency assessments and baseline studies for development planning purposes. Since livelihood zone boundaries are aligned wherever possible with lower-level administrative boundaries, population data tabulated according to these boundaries can be calculated for livelihood zones. These calculations can then be used as the sampling frame for household questionnaire surveys, for rapid assessments, and for livelihood-specific seasonal monitoring activities. They can form a basis for prioritising the needs of different parts of the country and for targeting assistance on a geographical basis.

FEWS NET has developed, for certain countries, a library of maps showing the relationship between livelihood zones and administrative boundaries at different levels. These are available on the FEWS NET website[43] and can be copied into reports or blown up to wall size.

The output from a livelihood zoning exercise is not just a map but a basic description of each zone, including information on:
- geography (topography, climate, soils)
- production systems (agricultural, pastoral)
- markets/trade (trade flows, including employment)
- hazards affecting the zone (drought, flood).

Livelihood zones can also be a useful starting point for livelihood-based project planning and management. The DFID Sustainable Livelihoods framework, for example, focuses on the five capitals (natural, physical, human, social and financial), which together determine the types of livelihood strategy that people are able to pursue. Many aspects of natural and physical capital are determined by geography, as encapsulated within a livelihood zone map.

Livelihood profiles

Livelihood profiles were designed by FEG/FEWS NET as a means of presenting all the relevant information gathered in a baseline assessment in an accessible way and in as little space as possible. The aim was to strike a balance between accessibility and level of detail, and to present sufficient information to allow a rounded and balanced view of livelihoods in different zones. The profiles provide a rapid introduction to 'how people live' in different zones.

A profile of one livelihood zone is usually around five pages long. It includes information on key markets, the seasonal calendar, the wealth breakdown, sources of cash, and the typical hazards and response strategies in this zone.

The profiles pack considerable information and analysis into a few pages of presentation. Therefore, they form a useful briefing for a newcomer who needs to get a quick grasp of food security conditions around the country. The geographical divisions are relatively small – as far as this is consistent with ground realities – so that the reader can take in the general pattern and the basic differences between areas and populations.

Baseline report

Baseline reports are lengthier documents including much more detail, and so are more suited to use for detailed planning or understanding by more technical staff. They represent an extremely rich source of information on livelihoods.

HEA databases

The baseline storage spreadsheet designed by FEG represents a useful storage mechanism for the considerable volume of HEA data that is collected in many countries (see section 4.2). This spreadsheet allows a wealth of data to be stored in an accessible and standard format, ensuring that the baseline data is reusable over several years. While this data is useful for the development of baseline analyses and profiles and, in conjunction with the analysis spreadsheets, for the development of scenarios indicating future access to food and cash, it also represents a very detailed and useful resource on livelihoods for researchers outside of HEA.

Appendix: HEA timeline

1973/74	Ethiopian and Sahel famines; post-famine assessments undertaken to integrate anthropometric and socio-economic information by those who go on to develop HEA.[44] Miller and Holt (1975)[45] report that: "People died in Ethiopia not because of an extreme shortage of food, i.e. famine, but because of an extreme shortage of money, i.e. poverty." Challenges the dominant focus on supply and food availability for explaining famine.
1981	Sen's entitlement theory published in *Poverty and famines*; this encourages a focus on food access. Practical efforts to understand access increases in second half of the 1980s.
c.1986	Ethiopian famine early warning system begins to incorporate 'coping mechanisms' in its monitoring system.
1991–93	Save the Children's post-conflict surveys in Ethiopia and Somaliland develop the concept of 'food economy'.[46]
1992	'Risk mapping' project starts at Save the Children in collaboration with FAO, based on food economy analysis (later called HEA).
Mid-1990s	NGOs (notably CARE) engage in livelihoods assessment and link it to food security.
1995	HEA taken up by Food Security Analysis Unit–Somalia, funded by European Commission. First operational HEA assessment and monitoring system established, in southern Sudan (WFP/Save the Children).
1998	FEG formed to promote HEA; Save the Children also continues promotion.
1999	Save the Children second staff to SADC to support use of HEA in vulnerability analysis in southern Africa.

continued opposite

APPENDIX: HEA TIMELINE

2000	Manual on HEA published by Save the Children.
	FEWS NET/USAID takes up HEA as its vulnerability assessment methodology through FEG.
	First HEA urban assessment (in Kosovo, for WFP).[47]
	'Food economy spreadsheet' developed by FEG (now the baseline storage sheet and analysis spreadsheets).
2002–04	First HEA-based food security projections for the whole of Malawi, Swaziland and Lesotho produced by national Vulnerability Assessment Committees.
2003	Integrated spreadsheet developed by FEG for analysis of impact across several livelihood zones.
	Individual Household Method of HEA piloted by Save the Children.
Mid-2000s	Growing dissatisfaction with 'emergency response' approach to food crises; increasing interest in social protection and disaster risk reduction. Increased development of HEA for non-emergency uses.
2006	Ethiopian government takes up HEA as the base methodology for the national early warning system.
	Oxfam GB adopts HEA as a core food security assessment methodology.

Endnotes

2 What is HEA?

[1] A Sen, *Poverty and Famines, An Essay on Entitlement and Deprivation*, Clarendon Press, Oxford, 1981.

[2] Malawi National Vulnerability Assessment Committee, *Food Security Monitoring Report*, Malawi NVAC, May 2004.

[3] J Jackson et al, *A rapid appraisal of the predictive performance of the 2005 annual VAC assessments in Lesotho and Malawi*, RHVP, 2006.

[4] RHVP leaflet, February 2006, at www.wahenga.net/indexphp/about_us/about_rhvp/

3 How has HEA been used?

[5] See note 2.

[6] FEWS NET/Consumer Council of Zimbabwe, *Harare Urban Vulnerability Assessment*, FEWS NET/CCZ, Harare, 2001.

[7] R Choularton, *Contingency planning and humanitarian action: a review of practice*, HPN Network Paper 59, Overseas Development Institute (ODI), London, 2007; FEWS NET/FEG, *Food aid targeting, preparedness and response planning – Implications of food economy baseline findings in the Limpopo River Basin Complex*, FEWS NET/FEG, 2001.

[8] M Lawrence and A King, *Serbia Food Economy Assessment*, March 2000, WFP, Serbia, 2000.

[9] J Darcy and C-A Hofmann, *According to Need? Needs assessment and decision-making in the humanitarian sector*, Humanitarian Policy Group Report 15, ODI, London, 2003.

[10] See note 9.

[11] Save the Children, *Rapid Livelihoods Assessment Report – The Impact of the Earthquake on Livelihoods in Muzaffarabad & Bagh Districts, Azad Jammu & Kashmir, Pakistan*, Save the Children/Thardeep Rural Development Programme, 2005.

[12] Save the Children, *Report on 4 Household Economy Assessments in Zimbabwe for the SADC-VAC and Zimbabwe VAC*, Save the Children, 2002.

[13] See note 12.

[14] Save the Children, *Household Economy Assessment Report – Thar Desert Livelihood Zone, Tharparkar District, Sindh Province, Pakistan*, Thardeep Rural Development Programme/Save the Children, 2005.

[15] T Boudreau and J Holt, *A Food Economy Report on the Ruba Lomine Project Area for Oxfam Canada and REST: a food economy baseline with an analysis of programme implications*, Oxfam-Canada/REST, 1999.

[16] HelpAge International, Save the Children, IDS, *Making Cash Count: Lessons from cash transfer schemes in east and southern Africa for supporting the most vulnerable children and households*, Save the Children, HelpAge International and Institute of Development Studies, 2006.

[17] Save the Children, *The Unbearable Cost of Illness. Poverty, ill-health and access to healthcare – evidence from Lindi Rural District, Tanzania*, Save the Children, 2005.

[18] S Levine and A Crosskey, *Household Economy Assessment of North East Turkana*, Oxfam GB-Kenya, 2006.

[19] H Kindness and C Chastre, *Trickle-up for a Change? The Role of Social Protection*, Save the Children, London, 2006.

[20] FEWS NET, *Livelihood Profiles – Djibouti*, FEWS NET, October 2004.

[21] See note 13.

[22] Save the Children, *Poverty and vulnerability in Singida Rural District. Household economy analysis*. Save the Children, Dar es Salaam, 2006.

[23] A King, *Macedonia Food Economy Assessment of Social Cases, June/July 2000*, WFP Macedonia, 2000.

[24] J Grillo and S J Browne, *Sekota Woreda Livelihoods Analysis, Market-led Livelihoods for Vulnerable Populations project*, USAID, 2005.

[25] FEWS NET/FEG, *Development Planning: Some Implications of food economy baseline findings in the Limpopo River Basin Complex*, FEWS NET/FEG, 2001.

4 How is HEA done?

[26] http://en.wikipedia.org/wiki/Qualitative_marketing_research, accessed 5 January 2007.

[27] Save the Children, 'Tackling extreme poverty – A role for cash transfers' (draft) 2007; Save the Children, *The Unbearable Cost of Illness. Poverty, ill-health and access to healthcare – evidence from Lindi Rural District, Tanzania*, Save the Children, 2005.

[28] See also J Seaman *et al, Report on a pilot project in Zambia to test the use of an extended version of the Household Economy Approach to provide information to support the design of Cash Transfer programmes*, 2006.

[29] For further information on IHM, see www.evidencefordevelopment.com

5 Is HEA reliable?

[30] In some cases, debt/credit or savings also need to be taken into account to ensure that income and expenditure are reconciled.

• THE HOUSEHOLD ECONOMY APPROACH

6 Looking forward and outward: links to other approaches and issues

[31] J Jackson *et al* (see note 3), p 10.

[32] S Levine and A Crosskey, *Can pastoralism be brought back to life? Towards a safety net and a way forward for North East Turkana*, Oxfam GB-Kenya, 2006; A De Matteis, *Market Functioning in Turkana District, Kenya*, Oxfam GB-Kenya, 2006.

[33] D Collinson *et al*, *Politically Informed Humanitarian Programming: Using A Political Economy Approach*, HPN Network Paper 41, ODI, London, 2002, p 1.

[34] For example, Save the Children and UNICEF are particularly concerned about the situation of children, while HelpAge or a government body dealing with old age pensions will want specific information on the elderly.

[35] But see 'HEA does not offer the disaggregated information necessary for social protection design or targeting', later in this chapter.

7 Limits and criticisms of HEA

[36] See, for example, Save the Children, *The Unbearable Cost of Illness. Poverty, ill-health and access to healthcare – evidence from Lindi Rural District, Tanzania*, Save the Children, 2005.

[37] See, for example, R Behnke *et al* (2007) 'Piloting the Productive Safety Net Programme in Pastoral Areas of Ethiopia. Revised programme proposal', report to the Food Security Co-ordination Bureau (FSCB) of the Ministry of Agriculture and Rural Development (MoARD) and the Pastoralist Task Force of the Productive Safety Net Programme (PSNP), pp 41–42.

8 What are the products of HEA and how can they be used?

[38] See www.fews.net/Alerts and www.fews.net/ExecBrief for examples.

[39] T Frankenberger *et al*, *Vulnerability Assessment Methodology Review Synthesis*. Commissioned by The Southern Africa Development Community: Food, Agriculture and Natural Resources, Regional Vulnerability Assessment Committee (SADC-FANR RVAC), 2005, p 21; see also J Jackson *et al* (see note 3), p 53.

[40] FEWS NET/FEG, *Food aid targeting, preparedness and response planning – Implications of food economy baseline findings in the Limpopo River Basin Complex*, FEWS NET/FEG, 2001; FEWS NET/FEG, *Development Planning: Some Implications of food economy baseline findings in the Limpopo River Basin Complex*, FEWS NET/FEG, 2001.

[41] H Kindness and C Chastre (see note 19); C Chastre and H Kindness, *Access to Primary Healthcare: Evidence from Singida Rural District*, Save the Children, London, 2006.

[42] See note 2.

[43] www.fews.net/livelihoods

Appendix: HEA timeline

[44] For example: J Seaman, J Holt and J Rivers, *Hararghe under Drought*, Addis Ababa, Ethiopian Relief and Rehabilitation Commission, 1974.

[45] D Miller and J Holt, 'The Ethiopian Famine', *Proceedings of the Nutrition Society*, 34, 1975, p 175.

[46] Including: J Holt and M Lawrence, *An End to Isolation: The Report of the Ogaden Needs Assessment Study*, 1991, *Making Ends Meet: A Survey of the Food Economy of the Ethiopian North-East Highlands*, 1993.

[47] J Holt and A King (2000).